Landmarks of Texas Architecture

Text by Lawrence W. Speck

Photographs by Richard Payne

Landmarks of Texas Architecture

University of Texas Press ⌄⌄ Austin

Copyright © 1986 by the University of Texas Press
All rights reserved
Printed in Japan

First edition, 1986

Requests for permission to reproduce material from this work
should be sent to:
    Permissions
    University of Texas Press
    Box 7819
    Austin, Texas 78713-7819

Library of Congress Cataloging-in-Publication Data

Speck, Lawrence W., 1949–
    Landmarks of Texas architecture.

    1. Architecture—Texas—Pictorial works.
2. Architecture—Texas—Addresses, essays, lectures.
I. Payne, Richard.   II. Title.
NA730.T5S64   1986   720′.9764   85-31497
ISBN 0-292-78074-5

Contents

Preface

This is primarily a *picture* book. Its being was provoked in large part by the pre-existence of a cohesive body of photographs by Richard Payne illustrating a sensibly selected sampling of Texas' best architecture. Those photographs were the product of an extensive effort on the part of Texas Society of Architects in 1983 to heighten public awareness of Texas' architectural heritage. That effort included the production of a traveling exhibit titled "Creating Tomorrow's Heritage" and the production of a short catalog for the exhibit which appeared in the December 1983 issue of *Texas Architect*.

Much of the credit for that effort by TSA must go to Larry Paul Fuller, who helped conceive the whole notion, organized and directed the process of building selection, and commissioned both the photography and the original catalog text. Additional credit is due Jerry L. Clement, then president of TSA, and Larry Good, chairman of the task force charged with overseeing the effort, as well as to Ray Bailey, Reagan George, Stan Haas, Tom McKittrick, Patsy Swank, Des Taylor, and Jack Tisdale, who were members of the task force.

Any selection process to determine twenty outstanding examples of architecture anywhere is bound to be fraught with controversy. Although advice for the selection was sought in a polling of practicing architects across Texas, the final determination in this instance was sensibly made by a panel of both academics and practitioners well versed in the subject matter. The selection jury was chaired by architect Ray Bailey of Houston and included architectural historian Blake Alexander of the University of Texas at Austin, William T. Cannady of Rice University, Larry Paul Fuller, then editor of *Texas Architect*, and architects Frank Welch of Midland and James Wiley of Dallas.

The committee's intention was to produce a list of buildings, well balanced in both time and geography, to represent the best of the state's building history. Most major periods of Texas' architectural development are represented—from Spanish Colonial to Greek Revival, to Victorian, to Modern. As political expediency might suggest, four of the selections are from Houston, four from Dallas, four from San Antonio, three from Austin, two from Galveston, one from Fort Worth, and two from smaller towns.

Contemporary buildings (i.e., buildings built since 1945) receive a lion's share of the list temporally. Although this period represents less than one-sixth of the total time period covered, more than one-third of the buildings included are post—World War II. The great boom of building in Texas during the last forty years probably justifies such a skewing by quantity of buildings represented, if not necessarily by quality.

It is interesting that the list, without particular intention, contains an even balance between buildings designed by in-state architects and out-of-state architects. Neglecting the missions (which could not really be called architect-designed), nine of the projects included were designed by out-of-state architects while eight

Supplemental funding for the photography and production of this book was contributed by Texas Architectural Foundation, a subsidiary of Texas Society of Architects, through a grant from the Moody Foundation. Funding was acquired by the TSA History of Texas Architecture Committee—Chairman: Graham B. Luhn; Members: Harold Box, Larry Paul Fuller, Morton L. Levy, Jr., Edward Mok, Boone Powell, Des M. Taylor, and Frank C. Welch. Special acknowledgment should be made for the efforts of the late Ed Mok, who contributed much to the work of this committee.

were designed by resident architects. The design for the other two must be considered joint design efforts by in-state and out-of-state collaborators.

The list is impressive, as well, for its balance and range of building types. Although there might be a temptation in such a selection to emphasize more "flashy" and visible building types, such as skyscrapers and public monuments, the list admirably contains not only these but also university buildings, recreational buildings, shopping centers, urban open spaces, and even single-family homes and industrial uses.

The selection jury itself represented a broad ideological background and the list reflects that breadth. There is no singular "direction" for Texas architecture established by the list. It is, like the body of work it represents, diverse and eclectic. Although I, as author, had nothing to do with selecting the buildings and would certainly have made some different choices myself, I have become more and more impressed by the selection jury's wisdom and even-handedness as I have worked with the list. It is a good set of choices.

The modest text of the book is not intended to be definitive in any sense. It is directed primarily to non-professional architecture aficionados, although the "design community" may find it enlightening as well. The commentary is divided into fairly independent "bite-sized chunks" which should make the book easy to dip into and dip out of. I hope it will yield easy reading for those interested simply in finding out more about the environment around them.

Although the text is short, it still required many hands and minds to produce. I am indebted to James Poteet and Jamie Lofgren for their help with research, to Patricia Henderson, Ann Loberg, and Mack White for their help with typing and editing, and especially to Susan Hoover, who researched, advised, edited, and organized for me on this project as she has on so many others. I am also thankful to Graham Luhn for coordinating work with Richard Payne and to Richard Payne himself for being so fast and cooperative.
                                                    L.W.S.

Introduction

What is *Texas* architecture? Has Texas produced built artifacts that express its rich and colorful history over the last 150 years and even before? Has this culture recorded in its buildings the values and aspirations as well as the circumstances and resources of its populace over time? Are there at least the roots of traditions of Texas architecture which appropriately bespeak the culture of the state and which might merit extension into the future?

This selection of twenty of Texas' proudest architectural achievements is a tiny sampling of the state's rich, but little-heralded, architectural heritage. The visual presentation of these buildings in Richard Payne's insightful photographs is evidence enough to any student of Texas culture that there are deep and meaningful tracks of our civilization in the state's built environment. In many ways, we are what we build, and in these artifacts can be seen not only the artistic aspirations of the "high" culture of the state but also the footprints of its everyday life. In the stones of the Alamo and the steel and glass of our downtown skyscrapers lie the silent embodiment of who we are and where we have been.

Geographically, historically, and demographically Texas is a rich and diverse place. It ranges from flat, hot, dry, and dusty in West Texas to lush, wet, green, and humid in the Piney Woods. It is tough and rugged in the Big Bend; gentle, fertile, and benign on the southeast prairies. The state has been governed by France, Spain, and Mexico as well as its own Republican government, the Confederacy, and the United States. It has been strongly affected by sizable immigrations of Anglo, German, Spanish, Mexican, French, Alsatian, and Black settlers as well as by "second-generation" immigrants from all over the world whose families came first to other parts of the United States and later gravitated to Texas.

This diversity of place and people has created a great range of architectural responses. Strains of Texas building may be appropriately tough, plain, and direct in one instance while wild, fanciful, and romantic in another. The simple pioneer ranch house in the Hill Country is no more quintessentially Texan than the eclectic turn-of-the-century palaces of Galveston. Both locally and statewide, there is seldom the consistency of style or visual character that results from more homogeneous physical and cultural determinants. Texas architecture is polyglot like Texas culture. It is a response to valid influences that range from local and indigenous to broad and universal. Its development has not been tidy, cohesive, or linear, and its environmental results have seldom been equally popular in all camps.

As early as the mid-nineteenth century the noted American landscape architect Frederick Law Olmsted found the state's environmental development a study in contrasts. In his book *A Journey through Texas*, which documents a six-month trek across the state, he admires the simple stone and wood homes, shops, and farm buildings of some communities while judging other environments he encounters to be "disagreeable in the extreme."

As recently as a decade ago, Olmsted's fellow New Yorker, Ada Louise Huxtable, then architecture critic for the *New York Times*, similarly experienced mixed reactions on a visit to the state. She observed "an exciting and disturbing place, a study in paradoxes." She christened Houston, perhaps prematurely, "*the* city of the second half of the 20th century . . . the American present and future," but found much to dislike in its "unabashed commercial eclecticism" (*New York Times*, February 15, 1976).

Texas architecture has not been nor is it likely to be in the future an easily digested whole. It is a series of vignettes loosely woven together in place and time. But if it lacks cohesiveness, it more than compensates with vitality. Variations in circumstance and background, coupled with the kind of freedom which heterogeneity breeds, have produced a lively climate for architectural development in Texas—a place where, in the absence of pat answers, interesting questions have been raised. The same freedom which has produced a dearth of cohesion has encouraged exploration and invention. The same disparities which have made tidy categorization of historical movements or periods difficult have led to some evocative hybrids— new and telling syntheses which are genuinely of their place.

At this point, Texas architecture is in its adolescence. The body of building and place making is now filled out enough to see some character emerging which is likely to be lasting. But the state and its environmental qualities are far from mature. Exploration, growth, and change are very much the order of the day. As with an adolescent child, we must be patient and understanding of the youthful excesses and awkwardness of our maturing progeny. But we must also be actively directing and nurturing—not with a vision of transforming this emerging being into some preconceived ideal, but working, with full understanding of its existing character, to bring Texas architecture to its own most productive fruition.

Landmarks of Texas Architecture

Five Missions

Between 1680 and 1793, thirty-six missions were founded by the Spanish across Texas. Under constant challenge from the Indians, the French, and the rugged living conditions afforded by the land, only a handful of these survived for any period of time. The most impressive of the survivors are a series of five missions strung along the banks of the San Antonio River within a twelve-mile radius of the city of San Antonio, founded in 1718.

The purpose of the missions was both civil and religious. The principal task of the missionary was to convert the pagan Indians to Christianity. But it was also his charge to raise the natives from what the Spanish considered to be a primitive state of culture to become civilized and responsible citizens of the Spanish empire. The missions were largely financed by the Spanish government but directed by Franciscan friars, an arrangement made possible by the union of church and state in Spain at the time. The sites held more than a church and a priest's house. They were tiny villages unto themselves with granary, offices, workshops, refectory, storerooms, stables, dwellings for the Indian neophytes, and quarters for a few soldiers all grouped, along with the religious buildings, around a central plaza and enclosed by a fortified wall.

Primarily oriented to the Coahuiltecan Indian tribes, the San Antonio missions were constantly harassed by Apache and Comanche challenges and were never able to congregate as many natives as did the later California missions, where as many as 2,000 Indians might be assembled. The San Antonio missions, even in their best days, never had more than 200 to 350 Indians in each of the five.

The Coahuiltecan Indians, unlike the Aztecs and Zapotecs in Mexico or the Pueblos in New Mexico, had no building techniques or traditions of their own. The sources for the architecture of the San Antonio

missions, therefore, lie basically in Spain. Skilled craftsmen were included among the early missionary founders and traveled from one mission to another in San Antonio, teaching the Indians their building methods.

The materials utilized were those readily at hand. San Antonio abounded in rich deposits of clay and building stone, much of which was available on the site or in nearby creek quarries. An impressive array of masonry forms were utilized in the construction of the missions. The rich local clays were baked in the hot sun to make adobe for walls and tiles for floors and caps. Irregular fieldstones of the area made up of granite, sandstone, limestone, and even slate were used in connection with adobe. A mixture of the two materials can often be found running randomly through the thickness of a single wall. Local limestone of two sorts was also quarried in nearby pits. The sandy, porous *tufa* was very soft and easy to cut but generally required plastering to create a wall impervious to the weather. A whiter, denser limestone, sometimes called Concepción Stone, was used for exposed façades and stone ornament. It had the very desirable trait of remaining fairly soft for some time after removal from the ground but hardening significantly after exposure to the elements. This stone did not split easily under the chisel, and fairly deep undercutting was possible. These qualities allowed craftsmen to produce the rich, variegated surfaces that so enrich the mission churches.

Wood was sparse in the area, especially when great lengths were required. Local oak was adequate for doors, paneling, stairsteps, and window lintels and frames. But it was more problematic where long spans were required, as in the churches. It was perhaps this inadequacy that provoked the friars to experiment with adobe and to create a new type of concrete made of pulverized stone, sand, and water mixed with

adobe, to be used where stress was not intense. The mixture was poured over wooden forms and hardened into monolithic surfaces such as the crossing dome of Mission Concepción.

Stylistically, the missions reflected two major influences, both of them imported from Spain. In terms of massing, the buildings were dominantly Romanesque with their barrel vaults, buttresses, and solid, geometric, low-lying forms—all expressing the heaviness of their masonry construction. The simple cruciform plan, used in varying forms in the missions, was also a legacy of the Spanish Romanesque.

In terms of ornament and decoration, however, the buildings were not Romanesque, but Moorish. The walls of the missions once abounded with lavish detail and brilliant color, only faintly evident today. Exotic patterns in burnt sienna, red, ochre, and cerulean blue stood in contrast to great stretches of plaster or stone walls left free of ornamentation. Doorways and window openings were favorite occasions for embellishments, as were the church interiors. Zigzag stripes, chevrons, corkscrews, painted tile, and stone patterns, as well as a few literal religious scenes, represented both a kind of decadent Spanish Baroque attitude toward ornamentation and a primitivism which resulted from their filtering through Mexico.

The degree to which missionaries, in a relatively short period of time, created such large and expressive buildings in a rugged new place is impressive indeed. Even in their weathered, remodeled, and unevenly restored state today, the missions still communicate much to us about the dedication, the values, and the lifestyles of Texas' earliest colonial inhabitants.

NOTE: Mission dates are from *A Catalog of Texas Properties in the National Register of Historic Places* (Austin: Texas Historical Commission, 1984).

The Alamo

1724 (present location), 1744, 1850, 1920

Mission San Antonio de Valero—the Alamo—is best known as a fortress rather than a church. It was, of course, the scene of the heroic thirteen-day battle in the winter of 1836 during which 188 Texas rebels fought the onslaught of Mexican General Antonio López de Santa Anna and his army which ultimately numbered 5,000 men.

The chapel for the mission, which has become a poignant symbol of not only that battle but the entire Texas revolutionary movement, had a battered history even before 1836. Although other parts of the mission were built much earlier, the church in its current location was not begun until May 1744. Destroyed by a storm a few years later, it was not until the mid-1750's that the structure we know now was rebuilt. The date which can still be seen on the façade is 1757.

But the stone church of Mission San Antonio was never completed while the mission was in existence. When the famous battle was fought in 1836 the makeshift fortress consisted of thick walls which had only been completed up to the cornices. Still, it was a beautiful and well-crafted façade with four fine sculpture niches, one occupied by St. Francis, one by St. Dominic, and two still empty.

Damaged during the battle, the building sat largely untouched until 1849, when the U.S. Army built the familiar upper portion of the chapel façade. Used as a warehouse by the Army until it was purchased by the State of Texas in 1883, the modest stone structure has now become a prominent landmark in San Antonio and a potent symbol of its city and its state.

Mission Espada

1731–1745

The most remote of the San Antonio outposts, San Francisco de la Espada was for much of its history the most vulnerable of the missions. Protected by ramparts and a bastion with cannon holes at the base and musket holes about eight feet from the ground, the tiny compound survived constant raids by the Apaches and, later, the Comanches over almost a century.

The mission is best known today for its irrigation system, which is thought to be the oldest water system in the United States still in use. Its most significant building is the church, which is a simple edifice with little ornamentation. Its one very special glory is the entry portal, which is unmistakenly Moorish, having the shape and lines of the Alhambra.

After the failure of the mission in 1831, the compound's buildings fell into disrepair and by mid-century were little more than ruins. In 1858 Father Francis Bouchu, a young French priest recently arrived in Texas, took on Espada as his personal mission in life. Finding only the façade and rear wall of the church still standing, he rebuilt the side walls on the old foundations with his own hands. He roofed the structure, plastered and whitewashed the church's interior, laid a wooden floor, built a choir loft, and even personally crafted benches and kneelers. For almost half a century Father Bouchu bestowed his personal loving care on Mission San Francisco de la Espada and single-handedly saved it for future generations to know and enjoy.

Mission San Juan Capistrano

1731, ca. 1756 (church)

Accounts of Mission San Juan Capistrano in the eighteenth century describe its church as "neat and in good order, though it does not compare with those described [the churches of missions San Antonio, Concepción, and San José] as far as the building is concerned" (Morfi, *History of Texas, 1673–1779*). The chapel is very plain and simple in construction and represents a departure from earlier mission designs in Texas. Rather than having a separate tower, the church's east wall is simply penetrated in the gable by three arched openings wherein bells are suspended. The interior of the chapel is a long, thin rectangle, originally painted with bright Moorish decorations.

Between 1762 and 1789 a new and larger church was begun at San Juan Capistrano on the east side of the compound, opposite the existing chapel. Due to lack of Indian labor, however, construction was stopped and a grander church for the mission was never completed.

Mission Concepción

ca. 1731 (present location), 1740–1755

The Mission Nuestra Señora de la Purísima Concepción contained probably the most complete and traditional church of the five San Antonio missions. Its cruciform plan, twin bell towers, vaulted ceilings with a dome and cupola over the crossing, sacristy, baptistry, choir loft, and attached convent all place it within the best traditions of European church building. The location of the church in the center of the mission compound, surrounded by a plaza and ringed with Indian houses, gave focus and isolation to the sacred buildings.

The church's thick masonry rubble walls are faced with carefully worked cut stone. Between the towers on the front façade is an elaborately carved portal, and above it a niche originally for a statue of Mary Immaculate. The simple triangle above the portal is matched by similarly bold pyramids which cap the two towers. Currently very striking in its plain geometry, the façade would originally have been veiled in painted geometric design in very bright colors.

Mission San José

1740 (present location), 1768–1770

Known as "Queen of the Missions," San José is easily the most elaborate of the five San Antonio mission complexes. A visiting churchman of the late 18th century, Friar Morfi, noted of its dominant church, "This building, because of its size, good taste, and beauty, would grace a large city as a parish church" (Morfi, *History of Texas, 1673–1779*).

The mission compound was impressive as well. Stone walls enclosed a perfect square 200 *varas* (611 feet) on each side, with towers at the corners. On each of the four sides was an entry gate. A total of 350 resident Indians inhabited the mission at its peak of population in 1768. There were 84 Indian houses built of stone, with flat roofs and parapets. They were built around interior patios which contained ovens, flowing water from the irrigation ditches, and bathing pools.

Friar Gaspar José Solís, another eighteenth-century visitor to San José, wrote that "this mission is so pretty and in such a flourishing condition, both materially and spiritually, that I cannot find words or figures with which to express its beauty" (M. A. Halsig, *The Alamo Chain*, p. 94). Indeed, Friar Morfi, who had visited all of the frontier missions in America, described San José as "the first mission in America, not in point of time but in point of beauty, plan, and strength, so that there is not a presidio along the entire frontier line that can compare with it" (Morfi, *History of Texas, 1673–1779*).

Governor's Mansion

Abner H. Cook, master builder
1854–1856

One of the oldest and most distinguished state executive residences in the country, the Governor's Mansion is a delicate blend of frontier plainness and aspiring sophistication. Simple, but elegantly refined, the building stands not only as a telling essay on Texas culture in the mid-nineteenth century, but also as a repository of 130 years of social and political memories. It serves also as a fine example of the well-crafted, pattern-book-based design that brought refinement of proportion, line, and material usage to early Texas building.

The city of Austin was founded as the new capital of the Republic of Texas in 1839 amid some controversy about moving the seat of government to such a remote location on the "western frontier." Even when planning began for a new governor's residence in late 1853, significant opposition to the effort came from a contingent of East Texas legislators who disputed such an investment in a town whose future was uncertain, having only been designated as capital until 1870. The city was, in the 1850s, a small, rude village largely made up of clapboard-covered log houses. But Austin was growing both in size and in the permanence of its buildings, and the legislature was finally convinced by Governor Elisha M. Pease to invest in a substantial building which would indicate the state's commitment to Austin as its permanent capital city.

The fragility of this commitment to Austin in earlier years is evident in the character of the state's first executive mansion that the new building was to replace. Built in 1838, the building was a poorly constructed two-story frame structure with a dog-run splitting the house in half lengthwise. When Sam Houston became President of the Republic for the second time in 1841 he declined to live in the house because of its poor condition and stayed in a hotel instead.

Governor Pease seems largely responsible for the aspirations of the state to replace the earlier poor investment with a landmark building that had style as well as utility. Pease was a well-traveled man with an interest in architecture and a predilection for the then-popular Greek Revival style. He served personally on a three-man commission established by the legislature to oversee the building along with two fellow Greek Revival devotees—State Treasurer James H. Raymond and State Comptroller James B. Shaw.

At the time of the construction of the Governor's Mansion all three of the commissioners, Pease, Shaw, and Raymond, lived in houses built by Abner H. Cook, a prominent Austin citizen, well established at the time as a builder of fine homes. Cook, who had come to Austin in 1839 after working in Nashville, Tennessee, and Macon, Georgia, was a master builder well versed in the Greek Revival style. His knowledge was acquired not only from first-hand experience with fine buildings of the style in the Deep South, but also from standard guidebooks of the time on carpentry, building, and architecture such as those published by Asher Benjamin and Minard Lafever.

Cook had a substantial building operation including a brick kiln in Austin, a stone quarry, and part interest in a lumber mill in nearby Bastrop. As low bidder for the project, Cook was selected to build the Governor's Mansion in the summer of 1854. The bids had been based on drawings prepared by Richard Payne, an Austin architect and contractor who frequently worked with or for Cook. Thomas W. Ward, another architect, was paid a small consulting fee "for his time" later in the project as well.

The building that Cook built bore a strong resemblance to his prior residential work in Austin and especially to the Raymond House, the Shaw House, and the Neill-Cochran House. All of these had dominant two-story hexastyle porticos with heavy flat entablatures. The orders on the Governor's Mansion, as on the Raymond and Shaw homes, were Ionic and very similar to plates which appear in Benjamin's guidebooks. The notable "wheat sheaf" design of the balustrade, common to all of these houses, was a hallmark of Cook's Greek Revival work in Austin.

Although the original portion of the Governor's Mansion has had little structural alteration through the years, it would have *felt* very different than it does today when it was first occupied by Governor Pease in June 1856. Local reports at

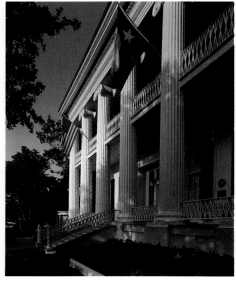

the time deemed it "just what a Republican Governor's house ought to be" (*Austin State Gazette*, August 18, 1855), and indeed it must have seemed a noble gesture rising above the raw little village of Austin at the time. It would have recalled the Jeffersonian advocacy of the Greek Revival style for Washington and especially for the President's House earlier in the century. It bore an even closer resemblance to The Hermitage in Nashville, the home of Andrew Jackson. It would have seemed American and Southern in tradition.

But there were hints of its Texas roots as well. Its sandstone-mottled local brick (originally unpainted) would have lent a rugged texture in contrast to the graceful lines and smooth surfaces of its white columns, balustrade, entablature, and trim. Its interior would have had a plain frontier feeling with wide halls, large simple rooms, white plastered ceilings and walls, understated classic trim, and natural Bastrop pine floors. Its straightforward plan and eastern orientation, surrounded by lawns and garden, would have made it a comfortable and pleasant residence well suited to its warm climate. The mansion spoke at once to the hardscrabble past and to the aspiring and cultivated future of the emerging state it represented at mid-century.

AUSTIN

State Capitol

Elijah E. Myers, architect
1882–1888

Across the lawn from the Governor's Mansion the old Greek Revival capitol building of 1853 was badly gutted by fire in 1881 and, with little regret, demolished to make way for a much larger and grander capitol building at the terminus of Congress Avenue. The first capitol had always been too small and timid to live up to its focal location in the city plan. The state resolved in its second effort to create a suitable crown for the capitol hill around which Austin was, by then, rapidly developing.

A competition process had, in fact, already been set into motion a year before the old capitol building burned, in which plans and specifications were solicited for a new building. Although the competition had been publicized in major newspapers nationwide, its naïve and demanding requirements resulted in only eleven entries. Aided by consulting architect Napoleon LeBrun of New York City, the Capitol Commission, sponsors of the competition, selected the entry by Elijah E. Myers of Detroit. Myers was immediately summoned to Austin, where, after agreeing to some modifications suggested by LeBrun, he was appointed design architect for the Texas State Capitol.

Myers was a fortuitous selection for the project. He was a prolific public building designer who built numerous courthouses and city halls in the Midwest, the Far West, and the South as well as state capitols in Michigan, Colorado, Idaho, Utah, and Texas. Forty-eight years old at the time he received the Texas commission, Myers had risen from a modest beginning as a Philadelphia carpenter to become one of the leading architects of America's Gilded Age.

Selection of a contractor for the project, like selection of the architect, was handled in an unconventional manner by the state's Capitol Commission. Payment was to be made in land, so that the award was given to the contractor who re-

quired the smallest quantity of three million acres of state land in the Panhandle that had been set aside by the legislature for the project. The commission received only two bids in response to their unusual terms, the lower one coming from Mattheas Schnell of Illinois, whose interest was more in the land than in the construction contract. After some negotiation, Abner Taylor of Taylor, Babcock, and Company in Chicago was brought into the deal to act as contractor of record. The land transfer and development resulting from the Capitol contract provoked a series of events that are at least as intriguing as the story of the Capitol itself—events which eventually included the creation of the famous XIT Ranch.

The construction of the capitol building was not a smooth process. Shortly after work began in late 1883 the state's superintendent on the project, R. L. Walker, complained that the local limestone that had been selected for the project was imbedded with pyrites (a pale yellow mineral commonly known as "fool's gold"), which would disintegrate when exposed to air and streak the cream-colored stone. The contractor subsequently submitted a sample of similar, but clearer, limestone from a quarry in Bedford, Indiana. This, however, was deemed unsuitable by Governor John Ireland, who insisted that such a selection would be contrary to the state's policy of using Texas materials wherever possible. The governor favored the use of Texas red granite, and popular sentiment supported his opinion.

The contractor estimated that use of the much harder and more difficult-to-work granite would cost an additional $613,865, or 20 percent more than the original bid for the building. No such funds being available, the legislature was called into special session but adjourned without making an additional appropriation. A compromise was finally reached when, in mid-July 1885,

the contractor proposed to build the building of granite if the state would furnish a quarry free of cost and provide convict manpower to operate it. In addition he asked that three porticos be eliminated from the design and that detailing of the stone be simplified to reflect the change of material. The state agreed to the terms and Myers begrudgingly made the necessary design changes in early 1885, changing the orders of the building from the complex Corinthian to a simpler modified Doric.

The state and Myers, during the same period as the stone controversy, began to have a falling-out. The contractor complained in early 1885 that there were defects in the plans as drawn. Unpleasant accusations were exchanged between the state and its architect, which led to visits by Myers to the job site and eventual deviations from the original drawings. Additional complaints continued to surface, and in February 1886 the Capitol Commission charged Myers with a long list of defects, evasions, and questionable motives, listing nine items in his plans which were deemed to be "either impractical, insufficient, defective or unsafe." The attorney-general was directed to place Myers' bond in suit, and the architect's involvement with the project was terminated.

Despite these and other problems, involving labor disputes, structural redesign of the dome, and complaints against the contractor on completion over roof leaks and basement drainage, the building was accepted by the state and dedicated on May 18, 1888. The result of seven years of strained relationships was a magnificent edifice which immediately became a great credit to its creators. The populace of the state received it warmly, charmed by its classic configuration, its elegant proportions, its massive, rusticated walls, and its dramatic balconied rotunda. Much to his Texas hosts' satisfaction, magnate Jay Gould deemed it "the finest building in the

world—certainly the finest I have ever seen" when he visited Austin shortly after its completion (*Southwestern Historical Quarterly*, January 1955, p. 427).

Temple Houston, Sam Houston's son, noted at the Capitol dedication that "the architecture of a civilization is its most enduring feature, and by this structure shall Texas transmit herself to posterity" (Texas Legislative Council, *The Texas Capitol, Symbol of Accomplishment*, 1967, p. 64). Judging by the building's endurance as a potent symbol of the state for a full century, his prediction seems likely to prove true.

Old Red ASHBEL SMITH BUILDING UNIVERSITY OF TEXAS MEDICAL SCHOOL, GALVESTON

Nicholas J. Clayton, architect
1889, 1900

Nowhere was the rising affluence of Texas in the late nineteenth century more evident than in Galveston, dubbed at the time "Queen City of the Gulf." All of the promise and prosperity of blossoming American capitalism were here, fed by a booming port that had become the gateway to the New West. Heady Galveston was ready to tear down its modest frame structures and rebuild in brick and stone to show its sister ports of Boston, New Orleans, and New York that this Texas lady had come of age.

When Nicholas J. Clayton arrived in Galveston in the winter of 1872, the city was embarking on this new surge. Irish by birth, but raised by his widowed mother in Cincinnati, Clayton came to the city to supervise construction of the showy new First Presbyterian Church designed by his employer—the Memphis architectural firm of Jones and Baldwin. Within a few years, he set up his own firm, becoming one of the first professional architects to establish a practice in Texas.

Over the next three decades Clayton's work and influence would dominate the physical character of Galveston. During his career, he would be involved in almost two hundred building projects in Galveston alone, including at least twelve churches, six major public schools, the Post Office and Federal Building, the Santa Fe Union Depot, and numerous hotels, homes, banks, and business offices. On one street alone, The Strand (the heart of commercial Galveston), fifteen buildings are credited to Clayton.

Sadly, only fifty or so Clayton buildings remain in Galveston today. Some were destroyed in the great fire of November 1885 that wiped out forty-five blocks of the city. The flamboyant Beach Hotel burned to the ground in a similar heartbreaking conflagration while Clayton watched from his bed in 1898. But it was the disastrous hurricane of 1900 that took the greatest toll of Clayton buildings. The majestic

Sacred Heart Church, completed only seven years earlier and touted as the largest church building in the Southwest, was so severely damaged that it had to be demolished. Much of Clayton's other work, though very substantially built, was also severely damaged or destroyed.

The storm of 1900 broke the spirit of Galveston and forced it to retrench from its position as the leading commercial and business center in the state. At the turn of the century the storm, as well as personal financial reversals, also struck a blow to Clayton from which he never fully recovered. Although he continued to practice architecture in Galveston until his death in 1916, it is his work of the 1880s and 1890s for which he is most remembered.

One of Clayton's largest and most prestigious commissions of that era was the design of a new building for the University of Texas Medical School in Galveston. The building resulting from this important commission is a muscular and wildly ornamented red brick and limestone structure, known over the years as "Old Red." It is a parvenu pile of unrestrained invention, mixing Romanesque arcades with Spanish Baroque parapets, Italian Gothic gables, and vaguely Moorish pinna-

cles. Layered onto a robust massing and rendered in seemingly endless inventions of stone and brick patterning, the disparate styles are as compatible as the Greeks, Turks, Scandinavians, Germans, Spaniards, and Anglos who rubbed shoulders in Galveston bars at the time.

The eclectic combination of forms in "Old Red" was common in the late Victorian era. But the building is progressive for its time in the classical and orderly arrangement of its disparate parts. In a period with a strong predilection for picturesque massing, the building distinguishes itself with a bold, unflinching bilateral symmetry. Its flamboyant parts are disciplined by repetition, rhythm, and massive scale. The huge two-story arcade that wraps completely around the building and binds it together owes a probable debt to H. H. Richardson's Cheney Block in Boston of 1875, although its use here is much more extensive.

The texturing of "Old Red" is truly remarkable. Galveston, as a port city, had collected a fine corps of masons and bricklayers who had immigrated from Western Europe. Clayton took full advantage of their skills here, requiring layer after layer of arches, corbels, brick dentils, and angled bond. The master brick mason on the job was Clayton's favorite, Denny Devlin, who also laid the even more elaborate brickwork of the Ursuline Convent a few years later.

The interior of the building incorporated all of the most progressive features of medical institution design of the day, including skylighted dissection laboratories and large amphitheatres. But, alas, rapidly changing medical technology and facility requirements through the years have rendered many of its spaces obsolete today. Although it is still owned by the University of Texas Medical School, it has suffered years of disuse and neglect. Its surroundings have been altered radically as well, leaving little support for the grand old vestige which once lorded over its end of a booming island.

The Bishop's Palace

Nicholas J. Clayton, architect
1887–1893

The captains of commerce and finance who led Galveston to its glory in the late nineteenth century created for themselves a striking collection of imposing homes built behind stately rows of palm trees in what is sometimes called Galveston's "Castle District." A few of the wealthy barons called in prestigious architects from outside the state to design their new palaces. Notably, Mr. and Mrs. George Sealy commissioned the famed New York firm of McKim, Mead, and White to design their home on Broadway now called "Open Gates."

But when Colonel Walter Gresham decided to build a home for himself farther down Broadway in 1886, he turned to prominent local architect Nicholas J. Clayton. Gresham was a colorful local attorney and one of the founders of the Gulf, Colorado, and Santa Fe Railroad. He had extensive cotton holdings and was a very wealthy man. Colonel Gresham intended to build the most elaborate house in Texas at the time. But he also needed a livable home in which to raise his family of eleven and to house eleven household servants. He was successful on both counts.

Architect Clayton was never very happy with his client's choice of site. He considered the land insufficient to gracefully accommodate a structure that would need to be so large and imposing. Colonel Gresham owned land nearer the Gulf which Clayton preferred, but Gresham thought the Broadway location safer from a storm. Although the grounds do have a rather cramped feeling and it is difficult to view the building from far enough away to take it all in, Gresham, it seems, was wise to retain the location. His house was one of the few in Galveston which sustained hardly any damage in the 1900 storm.

Stylistically, the house is eclectic High Victorian. It contains bits of the French Renaissance in its roofs, a large dose of Richardsonian Romanesque in windows and arcades, and a dollop of East Coast Shingle and Stick Style in its overall massing. The porches are safely Galveston nineteenth-century ironwork but with a touch of French New Orleans flavor. The chimney pots and ornament play the field entirely with motifs ranging from Moorish to Neo-Gothic to Tudor.

The exterior materials of the house are largely native Texas stone. The cream-colored limestone as well as the pink and grey granite was quarried near Marble Falls. Clayton had trained for a year in Cincinnati as a stonecutter before becoming an architect and had gathered a fine group of craftsmen to execute his often elaborate stonework designs in Galveston. One of his favorite masons, John O'Brien, cut the stone for the Gresham house in a small workshop set up on the job site. The exterior stonework here is unusual, even for Clayton. It varies widely, from ornately shaped trimwork to rugged split ashlar to irregular granite rocks. The result is much freer and less geometrical than most other Clayton masonry.

The almost compulsive variation of material and texture on the outside is modest, however, compared to the interior. Clayton was heavily involved in the design of the major spaces of the Gresham House even down to the selection of furniture. Each of the downstairs rooms is lined with a different wood—the front parlor with Santo Domingo mahogany, the library with black walnut, the music room with white mahogany, the dining room with antique oak, etc. The paneling in all of these rooms was hand carved, often to match a fireplace piece bought especially for the room. The front parlor fireplace, for example, was purchased in 1876 at the Philadelphia World's Fair, where it had won a first prize. The fireplace in the music room similarly came from the New Orlean's World's Fair of 1886. It is Mexican onyx and cost $10,000 even in 1886.

Interior finish materials were very carefully selected and came from all over the world—marble from Italy and Africa, exotic woods from the South Seas and Central America, porcelain from England, mirrors from France, handblown glass from Venice, tile from Holland, cherrywood, maple, and ash from Vermont, cypress and fine-grained pine from the Big Thicket of East Texas, Louisiana, and Florida. Shipping into Galveston was easy and inexpensive in those days when even heavy materials could be charged as ship ballast coming from ports which needed Galveston's plentiful cotton.

Many surfaces of the house were richly painted or stenciled. Mrs. Gresham, quite an accomplished artist herself, painted a number of murals in the house—notably one on the ceiling of the dining room depicting her nine children as angels.

The house is an eclectic showplace but, as previously mentioned, it also shows enormous concern for the everyday life of the family which inhabited it. Materials were durable as well as beautiful, and numerous clever inventions by Clayton added to the commodity of the house as a home. Ventilation, for example, is exquisitely handled to allow every available Gulf breeze to penetrate the house, sometimes even via internal passages. Floor-length double-hung windows in fifteen-foot-high rooms not only provide an extra quantity of ventilation by their size but also serve as doors allowing free passage out to porches and balconies. Carefully detailed shutters fold into the wall, again for maximum air circulation as well as to prevent banging in the breeze. The house was one of the first in the region to be fully equipped for gas and electric fixtures throughout and had such other conveniences as adjustable bookshelves and sliding glass doors well before their time.

The Gresham family sold their prized palace to the Catholic Diocese of Galveston in 1923, when it became the home of Bishop Christopher E. Byrne. It was during his almost thirty-year residence there that it got its current name, the "Bishop's Palace." The building is still owned by the Catholic Church, which has kept it beautifully intact for the past half-century.

Ellis County Courthouse   WAXAHACHIE

James Riely Gordon, architect
1894–1896 (?)

Some of the finest jewels of Texas architecture reside in its small towns. Often little known outside their immediate communities, these buildings represent the ambitious aspirations and strong community spirit which has characterized rural Texas throughout its history. Agricultural life on the Texas prairie was a tough and rugged existence requiring firm resolve and a strong will. Settlers of rural Texas were seldom "your tired, your poor, your huddled masses" but rather a restless, independent, strong-willed breed who fought to tame a vast, indomitable land.

The architectural expression which emerged from this life matched the boldness and audacity of its inhabitants. Powerful, permanent structures not only reflected the tenacity and commitment of the populace but also reinforced the community resolve by staking a visible, lasting claim on the landscape.

No rural building type exhibits this spirit more clearly than the county courthouses which sprouted all over the state in the late nineteenth century. Spurred by an 1881 act of the Texas legislature which authorized the issuance of bonds to finance such public works, many Texas counties seized the opportunity to upgrade existing facilities to match the heightened aspirations of their communities.

The extraordinary Ellis County Courthouse in Waxahachie is the result of one such instance. The

county, located just south of Dallas, had dubbed itself at the time "Queen Cotton County of the World," but when planning began for the new building in 1894 the price of cotton was only four or five cents a pound and times were hard for farmers in the region. Newspaper accounts of the time document the impressive resolve of local leaders to build "a courthouse second to none, in point of beauty and architectural splendor" in spite of hard times.

The architect chosen for this ambitious enterprise was James Riely Gordon, an aspiring young San Antonio architect who was only thirty-one years old at the time of his commission. Marked for distinction by his triumph in a national competition for the Bexar County Courthouse three years earlier, Gordon was working on several other courthouses at the time and would eventually build sixteen such edifices in Texas and over sixty across the nation.

The Ellis County Courthouse is the most refined of a series of courthouses Gordon designed in the 1890s which were based on a cruciform plan with diagonal entrances. The prototype was designed to fit the typical Texas courthouse site, a central square city block surrounded by commercial buildings on all four sides. The scheme responded to the hot Texas climate by placing an open air shaft at the center of its cruciform composition. The shaft, with staircase below and a tower above, drew air through the surrounding offices and chambers and exhausted it out the top of the building.

The visual character of these Gordon courthouses was exuberant and eclectic. The Waxahachie confection has been variously termed Spanish, Venetian, Romanesque, Byzantine, Moorish, and Victorian. It owes an obvious debt in its geometric masonry forms, round arches, towers, turrets, and carved ornament to the particular brand of Romanesque architecture which H. H. Richardson

IN HONOR OF
THE DEAD AND LIVING
OF ELLIS COUNTY,
WHO WORE THE GRAY.
BANNERS MAY BE FURLED,
BUT HEROISM LIVES
FOREVER.
ERECTED BY THE
DAUGHTERS OF THE
CONFEDERACY

had revived in his Trinity Church in Boston in 1873–1877. But the Gordon version is more intricate and playful than Richardson's work and has a broader source of architectural detail. Here, the geometry is looser and more complex, and the applied ornament less systematic and traditional.

The Ellis County citizenry took great pride in the quality of construction utilized in their courthouse. The three-foot-thick masonry walls are made of the finest Texas building stone available at the time laid up in a rich pattern of colors and textures. The base is grey granite. The bulk of the walls are Texas pink granite from Burnet County similar to that used in the state capitol. Stringcourses and voussoirs are Pecos red sandstone, and smooth-finished columns are of both sandstone and granite. Porch floors are paved with two different grains of marble.

The split-face finish of the stone contributes a rugged, rough-edged quality to the building which makes it feel at home on the prairie. It is a simple, tough building from a distance. But close inspection reveals beautifully executed small-scale details. The carved stone ornament, which was crafted by three Italian stoneworkers brought over for the job, is whimsical and inventive and has been the source of numerous local legends. The building manages both the monumentality and the intimacy required of a "temple of justice" in a small agricultural community.

The degree to which the Waxahachie courthouse eloquently expresses a sense of its place is evident in several films based on agricultural life which have been shot in Waxahachie. In *Places in the Heart* in particular, the camera's eye dwells on the building repeatedly, finding in its rich forms and textures an analog for rural Texas life. The building truly speaks to us, even today, about the people and the ambitions which created it.

Battle Hall   OLD LIBRARY, UNIVERSITY OF TEXAS AT AUSTIN

Cass Gilbert, architect
1910

When Cass Gilbert first visited the University of Texas campus at the request of the university's regents in 1909, he found a motley collection of eight buildings of widely disparate styles and materials which the university had collected over its first quarter-century of existence. Although attempts had been made when new buildings were added in 1903 and 1909 to create a "general plan" for the campus, no satisfactory physical vision for the ambitious young university had yet emerged. Gilbert's acceptance of the commission to design a new university library in 1910 marked the beginning of a twelve-year period during which he created, as university architect, a successful image and character for the campus which remains pervasive today.

Fifty years old at the time of his appointment and just reaching the peak of his career, Gilbert had behind him such distinguished designs as the State Capitol of Minnesota and the U.S. Customs House in New York and was already at work on a comprehensive campus design project for the University of Minnesota. He was also immediate past president of the American Institute of Architects. Gilbert demanded of the regents and received free rein, not only to reject the various building styles extant on the campus at the time, but also to exclude the use of traditional local building motifs in favor of creating a new architectural expression not only for the campus, but also for the region.

Gilbert's library brought a new level of architectural sophistication to the state. In it, as well as in other designs he proposed for the campus, Gilbert introduced the timeless verities of the European Beaux-Arts. Battle Hall is a building steeped in tradition and precedent. It bears great similarity in general form and organization both to the Boston Public Library by McKim, Mead, and White of 1898 and to its predecessor, the Bibliothèque St.

Geneviève in Paris of 1850. Gilbert had worked for McKim, Mead, and White in his early career and had acquired, as Stanford White's assistant, an appreciation for the refinement and finesse of Beaux-Arts Classicism. Gilbert also knew firsthand from his extensive travels in Europe the roots of Beaux-Arts Classicism in the Renaissance, Greece, and Rome.

In its composition, its proportion, its use of materials, and its detail, Battle Hall shows the sure hand of a designer well versed in his craft. Its massive stone walls, graceful rhythm of arches, and broad hipped roof eschew novelty in favor of refinement. And yet the building is far from a cold academic replication. It draws broadly on a tradition which is rich and varied and which accommodates easily the inventions and modulations which Gilbert used to make Battle Hall both fresh and appropriate to its place.

The *University Record* of the time notes that Gilbert described the style used for the building as "modified Spanish Renaissance." It goes on to explain that the choice was "naturally induced by the Spanish influence in Texas, and, since it was originally developed in a country whose climate and atmosphere is similar to that of Texas it is altogether suitable to the local conditions." The building owes an apparent debt to the Merchant's Exchange Building in Saragossa in northeastern Spain, whose upper windows, roofline, and bracketed cornice are quite similar. And yet, in its proportion and its handling of materials, the building is more like a sixteenth-century Italian palazzo. Its dominant use of rich color in the painted wooden cornice and terra cotta medallions and window surrounds, however, does not derive from either the Spanish or the Italian precedents. And its primary building material, a warm cream-colored limestone, is strictly local, originating in nearby Cedar Park, Texas. In the end, Battle Hall is a co-

hesive synthesis of many sources woven together by their connections to a tradition which has existed for centuries and which, in Battle Hall, finds an appropriately Texan expression.

On its completion, the building immediately ingratiated itself with its public and became a model for subsequent campus building. As university architect, Gilbert drew plans for extensive development of the university's land based on the architectural character he had established in Battle Hall. He hoped, as he wrote in 1922, to "make the planning of the University of Texas one of the greatest works of my life, if not in fact the single greatest enterprise" (quoted in *Paul Cret at Texas* by Carol McMichael, 1983, p. 34). Unfortunately, funding for the master plan was not forthcoming, and only one other building besides Battle Hall was completed by Gilbert during his tenure with the university.

Gilbert's work to extend the qualities of Battle Hall to the rest of the campus, however, was not in vain. His successors as university architects—most notably Paul Cret in the 1930s—greatly respected Battle Hall and Gilbert's general notions for the development of the campus. Cret acknowledged, for example, in a 1933 "Report Accompanying the General Plan of Development," that the shape of his own central plaza was "governed by the old Library," and that his "first concern was to ensure this building a setting worthy of its merit." Cret successfully accomplished this and by the late 1930s the central campus had the strong cohesive character which it retains today and in which Battle Hall rests as a grand old dame surrounded and enhanced by her offspring.

Lovett Hall

Cram, Goodhue and Ferguson, architects
1909–1912

When Edgar Odell Lovett, the first president of Rice Institute (now Rice University), sought an architect to give physical shape to his recently founded institution in 1909, he searched for the best available talent in the country. In the end, he selected the Boston firm of Cram, Goodhue, and Ferguson, who were widely known and respected for their previous collegiate work at Princeton University, the United States Military Academy at West Point, and elsewhere. Ralph Adams Cram, who led the project for the firm, reports in his autobiography *My Life in Architecture* (1936) that they received the commission via a terse note which included the following: "We have, three miles outside of Houston, a tract of three hundred acres; it is fifty feet above sea level and fifty miles from the coast. . . . It is bare prairie land, with a few scrub oaks in one corner. We have a fund of 10 million dollars. . . . We have a Board of Trustees and a President and we should like you to be our architect."

The commission, which included development of the master plan for the campus and the design of all of the major buildings, began an association between Rice and the Cram firm that lasted for two decades, setting an environmental tone for the university which prevails even today. The campus' architectural character, most richly embodied in Lovett Hall, has become inseparably identified with its institution, inspiring a consistent desire over three-quarters of a century to retain this character and to adhere to at least the general inclinations of the original plan.

Cram's successful vision for Rice did not come, however, without some significant soul-searching. Cram was academically inclined and an intellectual. He was dedicated to a revival of the medieval cultural sphere, which he judged to represent a superior social ideal. This philosophy was reflected literally in his firm's work at Princeton

and West Point and in their numerous ecclesiastical projects in which they had evolved a cohesive contemporary expression of Gothic forms. When Cram's work was not Gothic, as at Sweet Briar College in Virginia, it tended to be similarly academic in whatever "style" seemed appropriate.

In Houston, however, Cram's autobiography notes that they were faced with "a level and stupid site— no historic or stylistic precedent (not even that of Old Mexico of which Texas had once been a part); no ideas imposed by President or Trustees. . . . On abstract principles, we were convinced that our own type of transmuted Gothic was the right thing; but in this particular case it was manifestly out of place, and for a dozen different reasons— as were all other styles. . . . Manifestly the only thing to do was to invent something approaching a new style."

To accomplish this, Cram drew on his extraordinary knowledge of the history of architecture across the globe. He sought an expression that would be "Southern in its spirit," one that would "look like a college, and one built in a warm climate." Like Cass Gilbert, working in Austin at the same time, he was drawn to Mediterranean sources for inspiration, but for Cram the sources were far more diverse and their combination more complex and eclectic.

Cram reports drawing on the architecture of Southern France, Italy, Dalmatia, the Peloponnesus, Byzantium, Anatolia, Syria, Sicily, and Spain with a "covert glance at the Moorish art of North Africa." In the exuberance of his combinations he is almost the equal of his Victorian predecessors in the state, Nicolas Clayton and James Riely Gordon. The tall arches, attenuated columns, striping and patterning in brick and stone, and overall Moorish feeling of Lovett Hall, in fact, give it a remarkable resemblance to Clayton's "Old Red" in nearby Galveston.

Whatever its sources at home or abroad, the final design for the campus and for Lovett Hall, its first building, was judged by President Lovett on its unveiling in 1909 to have "successfully imparted a distinctive quality which marks it as . . . American of the Southwest" (*Houston Daily Post*, December 5, 1909).

Lovett Hall, the university's administration building, is an unflinching anchor and focus for the Rice campus. Its grand sallyport marks a point of arrival and an introduction to the serene academic quadrangle which is the heart of the university. Its relatively more solid and severe east façade makes a strong, even monumental, gesture to the public, while the west façade, facing the quadrangle, is more delicate and penetrable, graced by a deep loggia on the ground floor. The building's plan, with library and faculty chamber flanking either side of the president's office in a strong central tower, is orderly and even "modern" in its match with the building's rigorous structural module.

But Lovett Hall's real glory is in its surface treatment—its rich combinations of rose-hued brick, exotically patterned marbles, warm colored tiles, and Texas pink granite. The building is rife with inventive detail from the brickwork's striking elaboration on Flemish bond with shiner courses and fat mortar joints to column capitals adorned with bug-eyed Rice owls. In its major interior surfaces as well as outside, Lovett Hall merits close inspection and delights with its grace, its finesse, its erudition, and its warmth.

Highland Park Village

Fooshee and Cheek, architects
1930–1931, 1935, 1947

Good design is too often judged to be a luxury, accessible only to high-dollar public projects, prestigious corporate ventures, well-endowed institutional buildings, or homes for the very rich. Highland Park Village contradicts this premise and demonstrates how quality architecture can enhance everyday life, providing a significant virtue for even the most humble of building types.

The town of Highland Park began as a typical upper-middle-class suburban real estate venture in the early decades of the twentieth century. Its developers, Hugh Prather, Sr., and Joseph Filippe, owned a 1,400-acre tract of land just north of Dallas which they declared to be a separate municipality and deed restricted heavily. The area was reached from Dallas by Preston

Road—the first paved street in Highland Park and one of Dallas' first major highways. The name of the development was a combination of "high land" and "park," indicative of the town's elevation (approximately 100 feet above that of Dallas) and of its "garden city" planning attitude which set aside 20 percent of the land for park space.

The location of the Dallas Country Club in Highland Park in 1911 added cachet to the northern prairie, and by the 1920s residential development in the town was expanding briskly. By the end of the decade it became apparent that a business district was going to be needed to serve the growing population. In 1929 Hugh Prather, Sr., one of the original developers, announced plans to build a "shopping village"

on Preston Road directly across the street from the first green of the Dallas Country Club golf course.

Prather took his new venture very seriously. After some preliminary planning, he and his architect, James B. Cheek, made a trip to the Barcelona International Exposition of 1929 to help them visualize and authenticate the atmosphere they wanted for the new center. The primary architectural attraction for them there was notably *not* the later-famous German Pavilion by Miës van der Rohe, but a popular series of hamlets, recreated on the fairgrounds to demonstrate typical Spanish vernacular styles. Cheek made sketches, and together, in Barcelona, he and Prather formulated a preliminary design for the development. On their return to the United States, the

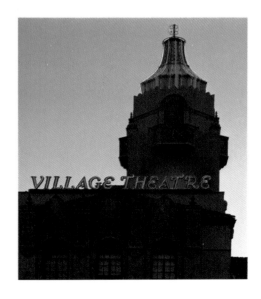

planners made a second pilgrimage, this time to southern California and to Mexico to study the currently popular "Mission Style" architecture. But they found it generally less inspiring than the Barcelona prototypes.

The architects and developers also investigated closely the "Country Club Plaza" shopping center, developed by J. C. Nichols several years earlier in Kansas City. This project was already being touted as the wave of the future and is now generally accepted to be the first example of the now ubiquitous shopping center building type.

Highland Park Village, however, made one significant alteration to the Kansas City precedent. Rather than facing stores to the street as Country Club Plaza had done, Highland Park Village was planned to face stores inward, toward parking

at its center. For this reason it was acknowledged by the Urban Land Institute and others as the first "self-contained" shopping center in the United States and, thus, the prototype for the modern suburban shopping center.

Six separate retail and office units as well as two gas stations were planned for the original Highland Park Village on 9.9 acres of land. The project was phased, with two units completed in 1931, two more in 1935, and the final two in 1947.

Initial marketing of the lease space was as innovative as the project's design. An elaborate model of the whole center was built at one-quarter-inch scale, using carefully crafted textures and colors to simulate the stucco surfaces, the tile roofs, the plateresque ornament, and even the *reja* grilles and balconies planned for the buildings.

Miniature automobiles and landscape elements were added for realism. The model, as well as close-up eye-level photos of it, was housed in a small temporary pavilion on the site even before the first permanent buildings were begun. This elaborate and expensive marketing mechanism was used to sell the *architectural* qualities of the place as one of the project's dominant assets.

The visual character of Highland Park Village has, since the project's inception, been an important part of its success. The stoutly constructed masonry buildings with plaster and stone exterior finishes give a feeling of permanence and quality. The gentle rhythm of arches, soft color and texture of clay tile roofs, and judicious enhancement through ornament and detail all contribute a charm that has endeared the center to its Highland Park community.

Though the town and the center have become somewhat more exclusive in recent years, Highland Park Village has been, for much of its history, a modest affair. The local A&P was one of its first tenants, and drugstores, a post office, barber and beauty shops, a local movie theatre, doctors' and dentists' clinics, etc., have long been its staple goods. A 7-Eleven arrived in 1953 and, refreshingly, Safeway is still one of the major tenants.

It is delightful to see such a convenient, congenially scaled, gentle and gracious built environment housing the necessary activities of everyday life. It is also instructive to observe its economic success and stability over its long tenure. At Highland Park Village, good architecture has served its investors as well as its users well.

Elbert Williams House   DALLAS

David R. Williams, architect
1932

The gracious Elbert Williams House in north Dallas was built as a *tour de force* of Texas regional expression in architecture, art, and craft. Its designer, David R. Williams, was the most prominent of a small group of self-styled artists and intellectuals who, in the 1920s and early 1930s, sought a particularly *Texan* expression in the arts. Their work, paralleled by similar interest in regional expressions both nationally and internationally in the period, sparked the first real re-evaluation of the history of architecture and building craft in the state and was directly responsible for the establishment of a consciousness of the need for preservation and restoration that has reached full bloom in recent years.

David Williams came by his interest in Texas tradition naturally. He was a fourth-generation Texan born on a cattle ranch in the northwest Panhandle in 1890. After his education in architecture at the University of Texas, he traveled widely for a number of years, living in Mexico, Paris, London, Rome, Florence, and New York. He returned to Texas in his early thirties and settled in Dallas. Shortly thereafter he began a series of pilgrimages across the state to view and photograph what he called "indigenous" Texas buildings. He was particularly attracted by the early homes constructed by German and Alsatian settlers in Central and Southwest Texas. He searched small towns like Castroville, Fredericksburg, and Salado for roots of Texas architecture from the early nineteenth century.

In an article in the *Southwest Review* in 1928, Williams declared, "Dropping into Castroville is finding peace." He observed that "In the many beautiful little houses left scattered over Texas by early settlers, there is full proof that some of our grandfathers and most of our great-grandfathers possessed the refined taste for which we have been searching abroad." He found that "The houses they made were nicely suited to their purpose. Built of native stone and clay and wood from the immediate locality, they seemed to grow out of the ground on which they stood; and they were beautiful because they were simple and natural, and because their builders were honest enough to be satisfied with beauty of line, and simplicity and delicacy of details."

Although Williams acknowledged the pioneers' debt to their native European backgrounds, he concluded that "these little houses are not French or Spanish or even English at all, but are natural, native Texas art, suited to our climate and indigenous to our soil. We should be very proud of them. We should use them as sources from which to draw a beautiful architecture which we could call our own and then invite the world to come and see." This is precisely the approach that Williams took in designing the Elbert Williams House. Most of the forms of the house are familiar to any student of pioneer Texas building. Specific precedents such as the Joseph Carle House in Castroville of 1840 are evident in the roof shapes, cantilevered porch, and general proportions. The house reinterprets the early Texas vocabulary, but in a literal way so as to pay due homage to its sources.

Williams had admired the Castroville houses for the way they had "shady places—wide verandahs and porches along the wings that run off to the rear on the west side, forming shady courts and little gardens full of flowers and potted plants." These traits were worked carefully into the Dallas house's plan. He also had high regard for the pioneer buildings' "slatted shutters which are closed into deep reveals of thick stone walls during the heat of the day to keep out the glare of the sun." These too were incorporated, although the masonry walls were brick rather than stone and the shutters were improved by mechanical operators.

The result of Williams' scholarly reinterpretations is a warm, gen-

erous home beautifully sited on a low bluff above a creek, carefully tailored to the needs of its original family of seven. The Z-shaped floor plan provides cross-ventilation and access to deep rear porches from lower-floor living spaces. Bedrooms above are tucked under the broad eaves, creating lively vaulted ceilings.

The house was originally imbued with a rich range of regionally inspired craft and detail. A Lone Star motif permeated the house, being used in a cut-out frieze on the front porch, with a rhythm of swags in the dining room, and in a series of threes above the living room doors as well as elsewhere. Furniture, lighting fixtures, and even rugs were designed by Williams and made on the premises. Lynn Ford crafted most of the furniture. Bub Merrick made lighting fixtures of hammered copper, tin, lead, or wood. Williams' regionalist cronies Jerry Bywaters and Thomas M. Stell created a mural above the living room fireplace depicting the history of Spanish missions in Texas. Native wildflowers were painted on the doors of the serving room and on other woodwork in the house.

Sadly stripped of most of its integral furniture and detail today, the house still retains its original warmth in the exposed brick and soft woods of its interiors. Clean lines, honest beamed ceilings, and generous proportions still bespeak the integrity and grace which Williams so admired in early Texas building and which he proudly extended to future generations. In the Elbert Williams House, David Williams clearly accomplished his goal of creating a "beautiful architecture which we could call our own."

Fair Park

George Dahl, executive architect
Paul Cret, design consultant
1935–1936

As time approached for Texas to celebrate the centennial of its independence, several cities vied for the honor of hosting a world's fair to commemorate the event. Although San Antonio, Austin, and Houston all offered greater historical claim to the occasion, Dallas offered more money and was designated the home of the Centennial Exposition a scant two years prior to the proposed opening date of summer 1936.

Dallas proposed to use the expanded site of the forty-eight-year-old Texas State Fair as grounds for the new exposition, but a completely new set of buildings were required. The city's typically ingenious financing scheme for the project, which combined municipal, state, federal, and private funds, was designed to produce not only temporary exhibition facilities but also a permanent cultural center for the city and expanded grounds for the continuing State Fair. The project was also seen as an economic stimulus to help pull Dallas out of its Depression doldrums.

Dallasite George Dahl was selected executive architect for the ambitious project with design assistance from the well-known Philadelphia architect Paul Cret. Cret had served, along with Raymond Hood, in a similar consulting capacity to the 1933 Century of Progress Exhibition in Chicago—aiding in site

planning, coordination of design, architect selection, and the actual design of the Science Hall. Cret had also been, since 1930, consulting architect to the University of Texas at Austin, where his master plan and numerous buildings were already well under way.

George Dahl, with the firm of Greene, La Roche, and Dahl, had also been heavily involved in work on the Austin campus. Dahl, a 1922 Harvard graduate, had come to Dallas from Los Angeles in 1926 and was already well respected in the city as an energetic young "go-getter." His vitality, motivational capability, and good humor were all to be tested to the limit in the tightly scheduled Fair Park project.

The design of the buildings at Fair Park reflects heavily the design trends of its era. It was, for Texas at the time, strikingly "Modern." The clean, planar architectural character is similar to that of several fair projects of the same period, notably the Stockholm Exposition of 1930 by Gunnar Asplund and the aforementioned Century of Progress of 1933 in Chicago. Its dramatic and much-touted floodlighting at night certainly had its origins in Albert Speer's blockbuster use of light in the German Pavilion at the Paris Exposition in 1925. But the site planning of the fairgrounds is notably un-modern for the era. Some parts of the plan reach back to the "White City" vision of the Chicago World's Fair of 1893 with its romantic lagoons and dazzling fountains. In other parts it is a rigorously Beaux-Arts scheme, injecting a powerful order and discipline into the large complex of buildings—characteristics that had been lacking in Chicago's more modern Century of Progress site plan.

The heart of Fair Park is the 1,500-foot-long Esplanade of State, which features an immense reflecting pool down its axis and is flanked by six monumental pavilions. The four courts established for the Centennial Exposition along the sides of the esplanade were elaborately landscaped to represent different sections of the state. The buildings to the north of the esplanade housed transportation exhibits while those to the south featured various other industries.

The focus of the esplanade is the grand Hall of State, a T-shaped building whose central concave feature, called the "Niche of Heroes," became a kind of logo for the original fair. Radiating from the niche are three wings. The front two originally housed regional halls, each devoted to one of the major sections of the state and terminated by the "Halls of the Centuries." At one end of the building the Hall of 1836 was decorated in early mission style, while the decorations of the Hall of 1936 at the other end were modern. A third wing, extending to the rear of the Niche of Heroes, housed the 200-foot-long Great Hall of Texas in which each of the six bays was devoted to one of the national flags that had flown over the state.

The Hall of State is still said to be the most expensive structure per square foot ever built in Dallas. Its exterior and many of its interior walls are handsomely worked fossiliferous Texas limestone. Its floors are largely marble of a wide variety of colors and grains. The building took

full advantage of the abundance and low expense of craftsmanship in the Depression era. Bas-reliefs, delicate metalwork, stenciling, and murals grace almost every surface of the building. Their themes are all stories of Texas, with an inventive panoply of regional motifs ranging from Lone Stars to cacti to oil wells. The names of Texas heroes are prominently featured along with high-minded words deemed to be descriptive of Texas history such as "Romance," "Fortune," "Adventure," and "Honor."

The architectural style of the Fair Park buildings, which George Dahl called "Modern, flavored with the condiments of Egypt and Archaic Greece, and finally seasoned with the warmth and sunshine of the Southwest," has gone in and out of favor over the years since 1936 (Dahl quoted by Priscilla Smith in an article in *Art Digest*, June 1, 1936). This factor, along with the dilapidation of the park's neighborhood and uneven use of its massive spaces, has contributed to an undervaluing of this important and cohesive period work. Fortunately, the recent revival of interest in Art Deco and Early Modern art, craft, and architecture seems to have assured the complex a safe immediate future and, it is to be hoped, a long life in commemoration of the state's first centennial celebration.

Paseo del Rio

Robert H. H. Hugman, concept architect
1938–1941

In September 1921 a disastrous flood ravaged downtown San Antonio. Water depth was measured at more than eight feet on some downtown streets. Over fifty people were killed and property damage totaled more than $50 million. Public outcry demanded that a solution be found. San Antonio would double its population in the decade of the 1920s, and the growing city keenly felt the need to heal the recurring sore created by the meandering little river that ran through its core.

Largely hidden from view, the river was lined at the time by deteriorating buildings that mostly addressed it with their backsides. Its banks were littered and unkempt and its water often polluted. Most downtown inhabitants considered the river a nuisance. It was no surprise, therefore, that the engineering firm hired by the City of San Antonio to propose solutions to the flood problem recommended that certain channels of the river be concreted and that the Horseshoe Bend area, now known as the Paseo del Rio, be filled in.

The recommendations, however, met stiff opposition not only from the always watchful San Antonio Conservation Society but also from the influential City Federation of Women's Clubs. The groups lobbied to save their "lovely winding San Antonio River" but required an alternative plan in order to deter the city from following its engineers' recommendations. In June 1929 such an alternative was proposed in a meeting of city officials, property owners, and civic leaders arranged by the Conservation Society. In that meeting a twenty-seven-year-old architect named Robert H. H. Hugman outlined a vision for the area which combined romance and nostalgia with promotional good sense and predicted the beautiful and evocative Paseo del Rio as we know it today.

Hugman wove a tale at the meeting of "old cities in Spain, of a narrow winding street barred to vehicular traffic yet holding the best shops, clubs, banks and cafes; prosperous, yet alluring with its shadowed doorways and quaint atmosphere" (quote in *A Dream Come True: Robert H. H. Hugman and the San Antonio River Walk*, 1983, p. 34). He sought to convince property owners of the economic advantages such a plan would provide. He attempted to persuade the mayor and other government officials of the proposed development's contribution to San Antonio's growing tourist industry, especially by virtue of its close proximity to the Alamo. He appealed to conservationists to help keep the historic river path intact.

Hugman's proposal was well received, gaining the endorsement of numerous civic groups. In October 1929 the City Federation of Women's Clubs formally requested that the city hire Hugman to develop plans to beautify and develop the river. But funding was scarce, and no action was taken. It was not until December 1938, after almost ten years of lobbying, speaking to civic groups, writing newspaper articles, and calling on community business leaders, that Hugman was finally employed as architect of the San Antonio River beautification project.

Funding for the river project came largely from the federal Work Projects Administration (WPA), having been secured by the tireless efforts of local hotel owner Jack White. The river was drained and the channel was cleaned and deepened—a messy and tedious task accomplished largely by hand labor with shovels and wheelbarrows. A concerted effort was made to preserve the mature cypress trees that lined the river by covering exposed roots and watering them regularly. Additional cypress trees were brought in from the nearby Guadalupe River to supplement existing ones. In all, over 11,000 trees and shrubs were added to the banks of the river, including over 1,500 exotic banana trees.

Over the course of the two-and-a-half-year WPA river project, 8,500 feet of bank were improved, affecting twenty-one city blocks. Over 17,000 feet of river walks and sidewalks were built, as well as thirty-one stairways leading to the river

bank from twenty-one bridges. The craftsmanship in stone, brick, and concrete paving as well as in construction of benches, stairs, and bridges is skilled and inventive. Approximately one thousand workers were employed in the intentionally labor-intensive project.

Hugman's design work fulfills the promise of his seminal concept. Surfaces of the district are rich and tactile. Paths are gentle and graceful. Landscape is lush and sheltering. Unfortunately, however, due to political disagreements, Hugman was not allowed to see the beautification project to completion. In March 1940 he sadly turned over his plans for the San Antonio River to another architect, J. Fred Buenz, for the final year of supervision.

Since 1941 the Paseo del Rio has had a somewhat checkered history. In the early 1950s derelicts and vandals inhabited the river banks, giving the area a bad reputation that was difficult to overcome. In 1962 the River Walk District and the River

Walk Advisory Commissions were created to work with the Chamber of Commerce and the local chapter of the American Institute of Architects to prepare a developmental master plan for the river bend area. This led to a second major effort to enhance the river walk, initiated in early 1964.

It was during that campaign that the commercial and activity development of the river, which Hugman had included as an integral part of his initial vision almost forty years earlier, began to take firm root. Today, the Paseo del Rio is a linear paradise blending nature and commercial uses in a lush display of color, texture, activity, and aroma. Twenty feet below the noisy street, the river hosts an idyllic world of its own, giving special character to a city that once threatened its existence.

Chapel in the Woods

TEXAS WOMAN'S UNIVERSITY, DENTON

O'Neil Ford and Arch B. Swank, architects
1939

The growing desire in the 1930s for an architectural expression in Texas appropriate to its place is nowhere more evident than in the work of the young architect O'Neil Ford. A colleague and traveling companion of David R. Williams, Ford was an outspoken advocate of the same sort of unaffected simplicity based on pioneer values that the Elbert Williams house illustrates. But Ford was also an architect of very broad interests—in advancing technology, in craft, in construction, and in architectural history. A voracious reader and seeker, Ford absorbed a broad variety of architectural concerns and incorporated them into his work.

O'Neil Ford was born in 1905 in Pink Hill, Texas, a tiny whistle-stop town just south of the Oklahoma border. As a youth he worked as a carpenter in the West Texas oil fields before moving to Denton in 1924 to attend North Texas State Teachers College (now North Texas State University). After two years of college, during which he had also taken a correspondence course in drafting, he landed a job working for David Williams in Dallas. He and Williams were kindred souls, but the older Williams had been more places and seen much more of the world than Ford. Ford, on the other hand, reacquainted Williams with the power and beauty of his own home state and was largely responsible for initiating their pilgrimages to the small towns of Texas in search of an indigenous architectural expression.

Shortly after the Great Depression hit, Williams closed his design office and Ford set out on his own. During most of the 1930s Ford went where he could find good work—to New Orleans to work for the Southern Pine Association, to Georgia and Florida to manage government land planning projects, to Washington to work for the WPA, and finally back to Dallas in 1936 to work on the Centennial Celebration. During these years he had also managed to do a few small houses, one of them for Mary Marshall, director of the Art Department at Texas State College for Women (now Texas Woman's University) in Denton.

Marshall and others became involved at about that time in a proposal for a National Youth Administration project to build a nonsectarian chapel on the TSCW campus. Coincidentally, David R. Williams had just become National Deputy Director of the NYA, so that between Marshall and Williams, Ford had no trouble getting the job as architect for the new chapel.

The project was tailor-made for Ford and drew his best efforts from beginning to end. Ford had long been interested in crafts, using woodcarving and metalwork by his brother Lynn and weavings by his mother and sister in his previous house projects. The meager $25,000 budget for the chapel was barely enough for materials for the building, but its designation as an NYA project made available a small army of construction trainees. In addition, Ford and Marshall decided to involve art students heavily in both design and production of woodwork, mosaics, carpets, and especially stained glass. The building was designed to be very labor-intensive with the hand of developing young trainees evident at every point. Ford loved the idea of helping young people learn the building trades and found the whole process a "fine education for them, and for Arch Swank and me" (Ford, personal communication).

The resulting building is an impressive confluence of frontier simplicity, lingering Mediterranean ambiance, and hands-on craft and construction. Local brick and limestone are formed into simple masonry volumes that adopt the character rather than the specific forms of the early Texas buildings Ford so admired. To these plain-speaking elements a vaguely Romanesque romance is added by simple but traditional church motifs, popular at

the time among architects as diverse as Roland Coate and Ralph Adams Cram.

Inside, the hand labor of trainees and art students is highlighted in richly stenciled beams, delicate brass light fixtures, carefully patterned floors, and crafty wooden doors, altar pieces, and pew ends. But it is in the stained glass that the spirit and cooperation of the building's creators is most evident. Of the eleven large windows, eight deal with themes of professional women ministering to human needs in nursing, teaching, science, and social services as well as in speech, literature, dance, and music. The focal chancel window above the altar is dedicated to motherhood, while the

rose window opposite it has motifs derived from Texas wildflowers. The eleventh window, a small one in the vestibule, lovingly portrays the building of the chapel, giving credit to its donors, builders, and decorators.

The Chapel in the Woods was a labor of love, and it shows. Eleanor Roosevelt's attendance at its dedication in 1939 confirmed the noteworthiness of the process that brought builders, designers, and craftspersons into admirable mutual support. The result is a gentle, meaningful, and evocative architectural expression which tells us much, even today, about the values and character of its makers.

Trinity University

O'Neil Ford, Bartlett Cocke, and their respective firms,
joint venture architects
1948—1976

If you blur your eyes slightly it is easy to imagine the Trinity University campus as an inherited relic of marching time—a sensitive, piecemeal aggregation of buildings and spaces collected over several centuries by a rich, culturally eclectic city.

The campus is, of course, not old at all. It is, in fact, quite new, having been built from scratch in various phases from 1948 to 1976. But the beauty of the Trinity campus lies precisely in its ability to elude the restrictions of time—its capacity to incorporate multifarious architectural forms, techniques, issues, and approaches into a rich, vital, satisfying expression.

The diversity of the Trinity University campus is all the more impressive when one considers that it is the work of a single design team. Forty-six separate building projects constructed over a quarter of a century were all directed by a joint venture between two local San Antonio firms—the office of O'Neil Ford (O'Neil Ford and Associates; Ford and Rogers; Ford, Powell, and Carson) and the office of Bartlett Cocke.

It was a bold move on the part of the Trinity University Board of Trustees in 1948 to combine the risky young O'Neil Ford with the more proven Bartlett Cocke as their architectural team for a "start-from-scratch campus" on a difficult site. With the enlistment of William Wurster, then dean at M.I.T., as consultant, the stage was set for an innovative and imaginative design approach which would nevertheless be, in Ford's words, "in harmony with the site, preserving its beauty, utilizing its unique topography—not altering it except where absolutely necessary" (from the minutes of a meeting of the Trinity Board of Trustees Executive Committee, January 16, 1949).

The first Trinity buildings were elemental, almost prosaic essays in economy. The magic came in their

siting, which was dramatic without overpowering the drama of the site itself. Simple rectilinear forms were nestled among trees, tucked up against a quarry ledge, or perched prominently along the crest of a ridge.

Trinity trustee Tom Slick donated the use of his patent and hydraulic jacks to enable the early buildings to be erected by the innovative Youtz-Slick "lift-slab" method. Up to 165-ton floor slabs were poured one on top of the other on the ground, jacked to appropriate floor heights after curing, and welded into place on steel columns. Largely because of Slick's subsidy, the method proved very economical, but also very nerve-racking for both architects and university officials.

Ford liked to tell the story of the morning the first slab was raised, when Trinity President Monroe G. Everett insisted the two of them rush to stand under the slab as soon as it got six feet up. "If this thing falls," Everett reasoned, "we'll both be better off there" (Ford, personal communication).

Technical innovations called much attention to the early Trinity buildings in the architectural press. Not only the structural technique, but also its careful expression in architectural form won rave reviews. *Architectural Forum* noted in an early article on Trinity in August 1951, "There have been modern 'horizontal' buildings before, but none whose sheltering slabs sweep for such 'miles' without apparent support—at once so widely overhanging, so smoothly unencumbered by any sign of a beam, so saucily thin. There have been continuous glass walls but none being so expressively hung from above like a glass curtain, which this literally is."

The clean, well-crafted buildings acted as a counterpoint and foil to existing topography and vegetation. Their neat order gave discipline to the lacerating crags and gullies of the land. With careful, sympathetic planting, the rugged landscape became civilized, domesticized, but not violated.

By the early 1960s, with the campus already established, Trinity found it somewhat easier to raise funds for new construction and began to be able to build more than "cheap, ugly" buildings as Ford was fond of referring to the first-phase boxes. The Northrup Hall Addition (1963), Ruth Taylor Art Building (1963), T. Frank Murchison Tower (1964), Chapman Graduate Center (1964), and Moody Engineering Building (1964) took the simple massing, evocative siting, and careful detail of their predecessors and amplified them with a new expressiveness.

The apex of this era came in 1966 with the completion of the Margarite B. Parker Chapel at the physical as well as the spiritual heart of the campus. Here, simplicity and drama are married. The great central hall with its dramatic light and warm wood tones enriched by golden ceramic accents is a truly memorable space.

The chapel and the later Ruth Taylor Theatre (1966) and Laurie Auditorium (1971) stand out as perhaps the best individual buildings on the campus. Their embrace of the ever-present slope, their interweaving to create pleasantly scaled, habitable outdoor spaces, and their exquisite use of warm, humane materials distinguish them among college buildings on any campus.

There is a powerful caring evident in the building of Trinity University—caring about a rugged, characterful piece of land, caring about making the most of meager means in hard times, caring about the sensual pleasures available from sensitive use of light, texture, scale, and materials, and caring about the everyday interactions of people inhabiting a place.

Texas Instruments Semiconductor Building

O'Neil Ford and Richard S. Colley, architects
Arch B. Swank and Sam B. Zisman, associate architects
Felix Candela, shell consultant
1956—1958

By the mid-1950s, as evidenced by his early work at Trinity University, O'Neil Ford had reached his stride as a designer and was distinguishing himself as a leader among architects in the state. He had blended his deep-rooted appreciation of tradition with a hardheaded search for innovation and invention. Like others of the era, he was particularly interested in tinkering with structure and the construction process. He admired the bicycle-wheel roof which Edward Durrell Stone had used in the U.S. Pavilion at the Brussels World's Fair and later used it himself in La Villita Assembly Hall in San Antonio. He also watched with interest the work of Felix Candela and others in Mexico who were experimenting with thin shell concrete and particularly with structurally superior shapes like hyperbolic paraboloids. He used the Mexican architects as consultants, making very limited applications of their inventive work.

But Ford's real *tour de force* of invention in this period was the Texas Instruments Semiconductor Building in Dallas of 1956—1958. Here Ford, working with Richard Colley, Sam Zisman, and Arch Swank, produced probably his single most original building. He was challenged by a truly new set of environmental requirements demanded by the embryonic, but rapidly developing, semiconductor industry. At virtually every point in the building, conventions were re-examined with the goal of creating a pure response to the problem. Like the innovation-oriented engineers who were his clients, Ford took risks and broke new ground.

The Texas Instruments Semiconductor Building marked a far more extensive use of hyperbolic paraboloid roof shapes than Ford had ever attempted before. With a minimum of structural depth, the long-span system provided sixty-three-foot-square bays, while at the same time giving a modular identity to individual places within the vast structure.

Even more inventive than the roof system was the spanning system for the interstitial floor at TI. A nine-foot-high space-frame made of precast concrete tetrapods separated the lower floor, which housed offices and laboratories, from the soaring spaces on the upper floor, headquarters of manufacturing operations. The deep three-dimensional truss provided a floor-between-floors for the complicated servicing and mechanical equipment that TI required. Several years prior to Louis Kahn's more celebrated application of the same notion at Salk Institute, Ford and his colleagues had invented a fresh prototype for organizing the intricate new demands of a mid-twentieth-century research/manufacturing facility.

But innovation in the Semiconductor Building did not stop with its organizational diagram, its structural system, or its mechanical servicing. In detail the building is inventive too. Its marble cladding is attached by straightforward, but novel, X-shaped hangers at the corners of each slab, thus avoiding more conventional concealed connectors. The lighting in the upper floor spaces is an early application of high-intensity mercury vapor lamps. By bouncing the strong light off the interior of the warped hyperbolic paraboloid surfaces, an even, high foot-candle distribution is achieved in spaces where intricate manufacturing operations take place.

Such invention, however, did not overpower Ford's strong appreciation for what is common and traditional. The fresh new hyperbolic paraboloid forms, he found, could be combined to produce familiar, almost houselike shapes in composite. The repetitive system of work bays could be broken occasionally to create gracious, traditional internal patio courts. The ma-

terials used at TI are both ancient and new. A soft, buff-colored St. Joe brick is used in the courtyards against elegantly detailed three-story glass curtain walls. Pearl grey Georgia marble is hung against a frame of sleek, matte-finished stainless steel to produce both compatibility and contrast on the exterior.

This is gentle high-tech. The building eloquently expresses the nature and philosophy of its corporate client as well as, to some extent, the computer industry as a whole. The products manufactured here are innovative and futuristic, but the people who produce them place a premium on traditional values and a gentle, humane lifestyle. Plastic-clad workers assembling tiny transistors in dust-free workboxes un-

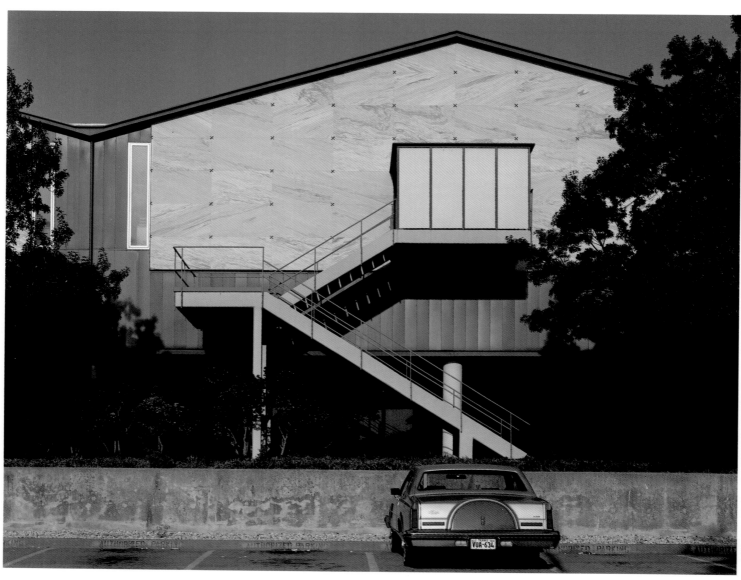

der sweeping hyperbolic paraboloid roofs are certainly an appropriate TI image. But no less appropriate are the lushly planted courtyards with rich, varied paving patterns, lively ceramic murals, and dappled natural light.

The most impressive characteristic of the Texas Instruments Semiconductor Building is not its innovative structural system or its novel mechanical servicing. Nor, on the other hand, is the building's magic concentrated in the warm, crafty lobby spaces or in the congenial patio courts. The building's greatest virtue is in the whole—the fact that it is at once both new *and* old, fresh *and* common, challenging *and* familiar.

Tenneco Building

Skidmore, Owings, and Merrill, architects
1962–1963

A few blocks from the Tenneco Building in downtown Houston sits the modest little Kellum-Noble House of 1851. Simple, clean, taut, and undecorated, the house is an elegant and unaffected response to mid-nineteenth-century residential needs. Its simple, squarish plan yields plain but flexible interior spaces. The deep double-decker porch that surrounds it on all four sides shields it from the hot Texas sun and also gives rhythm, grace, and deep shadow to enliven the building's volume. Highly revered and carefully preserved, the building has never been a flashy showpiece—rather a gentle, dignified building with great integrity and presence.

These are the virtues of the Tenneco Building as well. It is not a "blockbuster" or even an eye-grabber. It has never been a "dazzler" on the Houston skyline—not even before it was shrouded by so many taller neighbors. It is rather a sophisticated, carefully crafted representative of its ubiquitous building type. It is the finest of a genre of Modern office buildings that sprouted on Texas skylines in the decades following World War II.

Modernism is a style that began under the aegis of utilitarianism. It lauded economy of means and promoted a taste for simplicity, seeking "prudent" solutions to "problems" of its day. In the case of the Modern office building it sought to optimize—to produce maximum efficiency, maximum return on investments, minimum maintenance and operational costs, etc. But it also sought to be expressive—especially expressive of its rationality.

A key concern in the aesthetic of the Modern office building was articulation—articulation of space, articulation of structure, articulation of systems. The building was intended to explain itself to the rational viewer by means of often subtle distinctions and detail. Since real estate–based formulas often dictated the size and shape of the

building, the architects' efforts became focused on surface and structure. The period produced endless variations on the theme of the skin and bones of a building.

Skidmore, Owings, and Merrill, architects for the Tenneco Building, were the most prolific designers of major office structures of the era. The firm, comprised of over one thousand architects, engineers, and technicians in the heyday of Modernism, had three regional offices in New York, Chicago, and San Francisco. Although virtually all SOM work in the 1960s bore an identifiable "firm stamp," there were also significant differences among works of the regional offices. These differences can be seen in three office towers in Houston built over a ten-year span from 1961 to 1971—the First City National Bank by SOM/New York, the Tenneco Building by SOM/San Francisco, and One Shell Plaza by SOM/Chicago.

Characteristic of the work of the New York office, the First City National Bank of 1961 is the most abstract of the three buildings. It is an unadorned white structural cage with columns and beams of similar dimension creating a flush external grid. The glass wall is set back a few feet so that the cage stands free and clear. The building does not look "engineered" or even "built" and has a scaleless, unemotional quality.

Characteristic of the work of the Chicago office of SOM, One Shell Plaza of 1971 is the most structurally innovative of the three towers. It was, at the time of its construction, the tallest reinforced concrete building in the world. Its "tube within a tube" structural system marked it as one of a handful of SOM projects of the time that broke away from standard cage construction. The "muscular" articulation of its exterior tube gives the building a tough structural integrity.

The Tenneco Building by SOM/San Francisco lies between the other two towers in philosophy as well as in physical location and time. Like

the First City National Bank, Tenneco is a structural cage with recessed glass walls. Here, however, the cage is not abstract but carefully articulated to distinguish its parts and their various roles.

Columns are pulled slightly forward from the beams, accentuating a vertical line. Horizontal sun shades are clearly "hung" from structural beams above them. Dark "amber grey" aluminum cladding gives the cage a strong, tangible feel. Like One Shell Plaza, the building exudes a sense of structural integrity, but at Tenneco the expression is not "over-engineered" to the point that it seems more effort than the problem requires.

Tenneco's most dramatic formal gesture is to the streets which surround it. A deep three-story-high arcade is recessed into the building at the bottom to provide shaded "mini-plazas" on three sides and shelter for a drive-through bank on the fourth. A two-story interior banking facility is suspended in the arcade by means of bars in the curtain wall. The scale of the arcade is majestic—the proportion of the suspended element intensifying that scale by the contrast of low and high spaces.

The strength and simplicity of the Tenneco Building make it seem at home in Texas. It is not prissy or overly refined, but rather earthy and robust in a sophisticated way. The pervasive Texas pink granite paving on its ground level and its sensible use of sun shading throughout further tie it to its place. It is a consummate example of the Modern office tower sensitively and appropriately regionalized to Texas.

Kimbell Art Museum

Louis I. Kahn, architect
Preston M. Geren and Associates, associate architects
1968–1972

The story of the success of the Kimbell Art Museum begins, not with the hiring of its esteemed architect in 1967, but two years earlier when the trustees of the Kimbell Foundation appointed Dr. Richard F. Brown as director of the budding museum. Industrialist Kay Kimbell had bequeathed his personal collection of more than 350 art objects from which the museum's holdings would grow. He had also provided the capital funds necessary for a strong acquisitions program as well as a home for the museum. Brown's challenge from the trustees was to build both a collection and a building that would distinguish the Kimbell Art Museum as one of the finest institutions of its size in the country.

Brown had stipulated, before accepting the post of director, that he should have full control of architect selection and client input in the building's planning. In preparation for this task, he assembled a lengthy and detailed pre-architectural program which described specific qualities of the place he envisioned.

He understood his Fort Worth clientele well. He realized that a well-built, beautiful building which was, in itself, a work of art could be a drawing card—a powerful entree into the Texas art world. He knew that the most basic and potent appreciation of art derives from its appeal to people's senses. He observed, "The overwhelming percentage of people whom this building is intended to serve will not be art historians, other architects or progressive artists with a sophisticated background in architectural form. Their total experience of a visit to a museum should be one of warmth, mellowness, and even elegance. . . . A visitor to an art museum ought to be *charmed*; otherwise, why should we expect him to come?" (Brown, "Kimbell Art Museum Pre-architectural Program," June 1, 1966).

Brown drew a verbal picture that described an atypical museum for the times. He had rejected the bland box interiors of the recent Whitney Museum, the Los Angeles County Museum, and the Museum of Modern Art additions. He said, "Museum people have been after closed, dark rooms so they can paint the walls white, light them with artificial light, and control the situation. But by having control of the situation, they don't realize their system has control of them." He was adamant about the vital role of natural light, observing, "We are not after a measurable physical quantity, or a physiological reaction; we are after a psychological effect through which the museum visitor feels that both he and the art he came to see are still a part of the real, rotating, changeable world" ("Kahn's Museum: An Interview with Richard F. Brown," *Art in America*, September 1972, p. 45).

In the summer of 1966, pre-architectural program in hand, Richard Brown began to interview a distinguished list of architects for the job. He selected Louis I. Kahn because he thought Kahn would "approach the problem like Adam, for the first time." He found Kahn "willing to let the specific situation posed by the creation of a building guide him and tell him what the structure, engineering and esthetic ought to be" ("Kahn's Museum"). At least in this instance, it seems Brown was right. The Kimbell Museum pays startling allegiance not only to the director's well-defined program, but also to particulars of site, climate, and regional character. Its ruggedness, flatness, tawny naturalness of surface and color, and especially the way it copes with the sometimes brutal sun make it part and parcel of where it is.

In so responding to this specific situation, Kahn created a building that is something of an enigma relative to his other works. From his earliest conceptual sketches the scheme seemed to draw on previously untapped sources of form in Kahn. The repetitive series of linear vaults emerged quite early in what

was to be a long design process. Their origin is a point of considerable conjecture among Kimbell aficionados. Wherever they originated, it seems clear by their great success and sophistication that their selection was not meretricious. They are the essence of the building.

It is the vaults that give the building its loftiness as well as its intimacy; the vaults that light the space with their silvery, luminescent glow; the vaults that make the "rooms" of the building while at the same time providing the flexibility of uninterrupted clear spans. It is the nonhierarchical vaults that give the building its order and rhythm, injecting character into an otherwise undistinguished massing and solving the problem of the fifth façade, the roof, which is visible from the hill above.

It is the vaults that lock the building onto its site, paralleling a double row of former street trees that frame the museum park to the west. And it is the vaults, again, that open graciously to make a triple porch on the park façade, intimating the arcade of the trees a few yards away. The vaults, executed as they are in smooth, lustrous concrete, create a mystical presence in the building, generating a feeling of timelessness and peace. They are a magical device.

It is standing under one of those vaults that one can best sense the art and poetry of Louis Kahn—Kahn the philosopher, Kahn the mystic, Kahn the craftsman, Kahn the connoisseur, Kahn the architect. His was a sensual art, full of emotion and sentiment. He was a modern romantic. His Kimbell Art Museum speaks the language of human experience. It is a building to touch and feel—pocked satin of travertine alongside the mottled "liquid stone" of concrete, honey-colored oak against cool blue stainless steel —and everywhere a magic glow of light borrowed from the sun.

Museum of Fine Arts

Miës van der Rohe
1955–1956 (Cullinan Hall), 1972–1973 (Brown Pavilion)

When New York architect Ralph Adams Cram first visited the site assigned him for Rice University just south of Houston in 1909 he found a "level and stupid" site—277 acres of bare prairie land broken only by a few scrub oaks in one corner. A scant forty-five years later, when Chicago architect Miës van der Rohe first visited a site virtually across the street from Cram's which had been assigned him for extensions to the Museum of Fine Arts he found a very different situation indeed.

If Cram had been disturbed by a lack of context from which to draw inspiration, Miës could only have complained that there was so much context in 1954 that it demanded extraordinary skill to forge so many constraints into a satisfying building. But forge them he did, producing one of the most particular and responsive buildings of his very distinguished career.

In 1909 South Main Street was a narrow dirt road leading from the city into a vast undeveloped prairie to the south of Houston. After the decision was made to place the Rice campus along it, activity began immediately to plan the future, not only of the street itself, but also of the districts around it. In 1913 George E. Kessler of St. Louis, one of the most respected landscape architects of the day, was commissioned by the City of Houston to prepare a master plan for the development of South Main and for the 285-acre Hermann Park across the street from the Rice campus. There was a desire on the part of Rice trustees, city officials, and private developers in the area to establish a cohesive character for the district. The Kessler plan was intended to assure that solidarity.

One of Kessler's first gestures was to create an ellipse where Montrose Street angled into South Main at the northern end of the district and to use this ellipse as a spring-point for access into Hermann Park. Just north of the ellipse, in the gore created by South Main and Montrose, lay a triangular site which was designated as the location for the Museum of Fine Arts. The museum, in an effort to assure an architectural continuity which would complement the planning continuity in the district, chose as architect William Ward Watkins, who was then chairman of the Architecture Department at Rice and supervising architect for Rice buildings.

Watkins proposed a massive stone neoclassical block for the museum, a surprising counterpoint to the gentler, more picturesque work he and Cram had done elsewhere in the district. Built in two phases in 1924 and 1926, the U-shaped building addressed the Kessler ellipse boldly with a double-order Ionic colonnade. Two long wings behind were splayed to align with South Main and Montrose on either side.

Enter Miës van der Rohe. In 1954, at the peak of his career and well respected around the world, Miës had not yet built a single permanent public building. In 1942, with little real work to do, he had drawn a project for a Museum for a Small City. In it, Miës proposed a spatial solution which was the antithesis of traditional museum practice. In the place of an ordered progression of rooms where art is protected and contained, Miës proposed a free-flowing neutral space—visually and physically connected to the exterior. Here, he said, art would assume a new dimension as each art object related freely in space to other art objects as well as to the outside environment.

Miës applied this idea in an almost didactic way in his first-phase addition to the Houston museum, Cullinan Hall. Because the Watkins building was a typical cellular museum, the vast openness of the new Miës room provided a stark contrast and counterpoint.

Miës inserted Cullinan Hall directly into the courtyard formed by

the U-shape of the Watkins building. He spanned the space with deep steel girders which were exposed above the roof like those of his earlier Crown Hall at the Illinois Institute of Technology in Chicago. The new north façade was bowed to emphasize the fan shape of the site. Cullinan Hall was, at the time, the largest example of Miës' so-called "universal" space. Its floor-to-ceiling, north-facing glass wall made it seem truly vast as well as displaying its contents openly and tantalizingly to the public.

Cullinan Hall was the first phase of a master plan which Miës had prepared for the museum as part of his original commission. The construction of the Brown Pavilion in 1973 completed that master plan. As he had originally proposed, Miës added to his 1956 addition by creating a broad sweep of changing galleries across the entire north end of the site. Cullinan Hall was left intact, but its north-facing glass wall was removed to allow it to spill directly into the new spaces on two levels. The resulting split-level interaction between the new open lobby on the lower level, Cullinan Hall on a mid-level, and the vast Brown Galleries above offers a truly memorable spatial experience.

Trademark of Miës' work, the materials and details throughout the extensions are minimal and elegant. The steel, which was white in the Cullinan addition, was changed to black for the Brown Pavilion, giving it a more solid, if somewhat somber, feeling.

In the Museum of Fine Arts extensions Miës merges a rich but demanding history of site development with a revolutionary notion of museum display and manages to produce a seamless and cohesive whole. He draws a rather rigid existing building and a complex new museum program phased over a fifteen-year period into a clear, seemingly inevitable scheme. The clarity of the building amidst such formidable constraints demonstrates Miës' ex-

traordinary skill in distilling complex architectural variables into a simple but profound formal solution.

The end result is a building in which one can *feel* the sweep of the site and the place of the building in relation to surrounding streets and the ellipse—where one can *feel* the integral anchor of the original Watkins building and the splay of its early wings. Miës' museum in Houston is not just a "universal" statement such as we are accustomed to acknowledging in his work, but also a particular and sensitive reaction to the exigencies of its situation.

Pennzoil Place   HOUSTON

Philip Johnson and John Burgee, architects
S. I. Morris Associates, associate architect
1973–1975

No building in Texas has created more excitement in the process of its coming to being than Pennzoil Place did in Houston in the early 1970s. Already graced by such refined modern works as Miës' Museum of Fine Arts and SOM's Tenneco Building, Houston was ready to break away, to raise buildings which would reflect its ambitions and vitality. Pennzoil gave a palpable presence to the city's energies. Here was a building that expressed in physical form the free-wheeling, chance-taking, wildcatter character of Houston. It immediately became a symbol for the city and a sign of things to come for Texas commercial building.

Three major actors were responsible for the daring and the quality of Pennzoil Place—Pennzoil Board Chairman Hugh Liedtke, Houston developer Gerald D. Hines, and New York architect Philip Johnson. The building, as it stands, is a monument to the resolve of all three.

Liedtke and his company had made a decision in 1970 to consolidate their scattered offices in a centralized location in downtown Houston. Ill-equipped to plan and build the building itself, the Pennzoil company called on Hines' expertise as one of the largest developers in the country and one who was known for producing such quality Houston projects as One Shell Plaza and the Galleria Shopping Center. Liedtke made it clear to Hines that Pennzoil "didn't want 'just another building,' particularly a modern wedding cake or a cigar box" ("Is 'Wow!' Enough?" *Progressive Architecture*, August 1977, p. 66).

Hines called on iconoclast Philip Johnson and his partner John Burgee to produce an architectural expression which would satisfy Liedtke's desire for a distinctive, identity-producing building while at the same time satisfying his own financial requirements for the project. Pennzoil was to be the major and controlling tenant in the building, but it would require only half of

the 1.6 million square feet which economics dictated the site should bear. The remaining commercial lease space had to fit into the requirements of the speculative office market at the time.

Despite the project's requirement for high visibility and very high density, Johnson and Burgee came back to Hines and Liedtke with a solution that would notably *not* be the tallest building on the Houston skyline. They opted instead for an ingenious twin-tower scheme which, even though it covered almost three-quarters of the block with tower footprints, produced adequate light and view from all lease spaces. This was accomplished by slicing the buildings at 45° angles to create trapezoids in plan and placing them very close together— only ten feet apart at one point. The remainder of the block, outside the tower footprints, was to be covered with a sloping metal space frame and sheathed in glass to create two triangular atrium lobbies. The ten-foot space between the towers connected the lobbies to provide diagonal pedestrian access through the block, making at least a symbolic link between the downtown office buildings to the south of the project and Houston's cultural center and convention hall to the north.

A model of this scheme was presented to Liedtke, who liked the two-tower approach, the angles, and the sloping atrium units between the towers. But the model, at that point, had flat roofs. Liedtke said he wanted his project "to soar, to reach, and a flat-top doesn't reach." Johnson reportedly took one of the angled corner sections of the presentation model and set it on the roof, asking Liedtke if that was what he was talking about. And *voilà*—Pennzoil Place was born.

Of course, a great deal of refinement was necessary after that point in order to make walls turn gracefully into roofs and to make offices fit neatly under sloped edges. But the geometric scheme turned out to

be an inspired one. The final building form seems far more complex in experience than its plan would indicate. Like good minimalist sculpture, it makes visual puzzles for the viewer that are at once baffling and easy to decipher. As one moves around the building from a distance, its elements come together and then break apart, compose and

recompose in a dynamic, kinetic melody of form.

The building was immediately lauded as a marriage of "the art of architecture and the business of investment construction" (Ada Louise Huxtable, "Houston's Towering Achievement," *New York Times*, February 22, 1976). It became proof to skeptical high-art architects that a developer *could* be an enlightened client for innovative design and proof to developers that good design *could* pay off in the real estate marketplace.

Well beyond its immediate economic successes, Pennzoil Place has become a vital asset for the city of Houston. It is a colossal kaleidoscopic sculpture for the city, enhancing every freeway view of downtown that catches it. It has inspired a greater richness of form and shape in the buildings which have succeeded it, not only in Houston, but around the globe. It is one of a very few Texas buildings of world-class stature which can legitimately claim to have made a significant impact on the discipline of architecture worldwide.

San Antonio Museum of Art

Cambridge Seven Associates, architects
Chumney, Jones, and Kell, associate architects
1977–1981

The idea of converting a beer brewery into an art museum is tinged with an irresistible irony. The delicious antipathy of the two uses would, for most, render the idea of their sharing quarters improbable, even if the arrangement *were* to be sequential and not concurrent. San Antonio, thankfully, has never been a city to shy away from the improbable.

When existing quarters became unbearably tight at the eclectic Witte Museum in the summer of 1971, director Jack McGregor began beating the bushes in search of some way to gain new space for his expanding operation. Unlike many directors, who might have concentrated in such a situation on writing architectural programs and checking construction costs, McGregor took a broader view of his problem. "I know this doesn't sound very professional," he would confess later, "but I just wanted a *beautiful* building" (*San Antonio Express-News*, March 1, 1981).

So when McGregor literally stumbled across the derelict Lone Star Brewery with its majestic arched façades, soaring interior spaces, and handsome brick detail, he saw the potential for a marriage between high and low culture which resulted, ten years later, in the enormously successful San Antonio Museum of Art.

The old brewery building began its *first* life in 1903, when Adolphus Busch, the proud new owner of the Lone Star Brewing Company of San Antonio, replaced the firm's 1884 wooden brewhouse with a modern new masonry one. The solidly constructed, vaguely Romanesque fortress was designed by the St. Louis firm of Jugenfeld and Company, who made a specialty of brewery design. Newspaper reports at the time found it a "splendid building . . . No expense was spared in its architectural beauty" (quoted in the *San Antonio Light*, February 22, 1981). And, indeed, the building,

along with some ancillary structures, reportedly cost $1 million at the time.

Alas, the glory of the new "temple that beer built" was cut short when, a scant fifteen years later, the threat of prohibition forced its closing. Parts of the building were reopened as the Lone Star Cotton Mill and then the Lone Star Ice and Food Store in the 1920s, but neither of the operations could return the building to its former glory. For the next fifty years it would be parceled out to various enterprises, mostly as warehouse space.

Scarred, but still proud, the building offered other advantages besides its latent beauty to museum backers who viewed it in the early 1970s. Once considered remote from the city, the brewery building was now close to San Antonio's expanding downtown. Even more important, the San Antonio River formed the rear boundary of the property, thereby creating the potential for future links to the city's vital river system. The interiors were huge loft spaces with the long expanses of wall and high ceilings necessary for housing cereal cookers, mash tubs, fermenting tanks—and, coincidentally, works of art.

In 1972 the museum board purchased five of the old brewery buildings and asked a University of Texas architecture class to study their potential for adaptive re-use. The following year, the architectural firm Cambridge Seven Associates was hired as lead architects for the museum project. Peter Chermayeff, principal in charge of the design, was taken by the building's "character, grandness, power, and yes, humor and whimsy." He noted that "An architect today seldom has the opportunity to work with buildings of the scale of this one. The extravagance of space and volume is something you don't ordinarily have" (*San Antonio Express*, March 2, 1981).

The architects' design approach

was to conscientiously keep the building they were given, restoring its delicately castellated walls, its robust iron interior frame, and its concrete "washboard" vaults. But where interventions were necessary to make the facility a modern museum, no attempt was made to blend in with the original design. New stairtowers and "skywalk" on the exterior were rendered in a dark, sleek steel and smoked-glass vocabulary that sets them clearly apart from the rich brick texture and buff color of the original building. New skylights and penthouse pavilion got jagged saw-toothed forms which create a rather stark argument with the more sedate volumes on which they rest.

Inside, a crisp lining of plaster, glass, metal, wood, and slate creates a more sedate backdrop for art than the old exposed brick walls would have. But the eccentric original structural system is still there, admirably spared from camouflage by an ingenious air ducting system which runs in vertical chases between thick gallery walls.

Glamorous high-tech elevators are the *tour de force* of the interior, providing vertical circulation in each of the museum's towers. These "moving rooms" with a view afford a unique and tantalizing preview of the museum's contents as one moves through the building. Shaft and cab are glass-enclosed on three sides, with the fourth plane (the doors) being mirrored. The elevator workings—guidewheels and counterweights—are exposed and chrome finished. A grid of tiny lights above and below the cab announces its arrival and departure. The effect of the whole is that of a slow-moving kinetic sculpture which lumbers through the building bearing visitors to their desired destinations. It is beautiful *and* fun. It is an instant hit with new museum patrons.

The great virtue of the San Antonio Museum of Art lies in its appreciation of timeless values in architecture. It acknowledges those qualities in buildings, such as beauty, grace, and generosity of space, which transcend time and particular function. The building teaches the value of investment in these qualities in any generation, not only for immediate satisfaction, but also for the enrichment of generations to come.